MESSAGES FROM THE MERCY SEAT

REV. LEROY THOMPSON, PH.D.

Joshua Tree
Publishing
JoshuaTreePublishing.com

• Chicago •

MESSAGES FROM THE MERCY SEAT

Rev. LeRoy Thompson, Ph.D.

Published by

Joshua Tree Publishing
• Chicago •
JoshuaTreePublishing.com

13-Digit ISBN: 978-1-956823-22-6
                 978-0-9845904-6-9 (First Edition 2011)

Global Truth Ministries   globaltruth.us

All Bible verses are from King James Version (KJV) Public Domain

Disclaimer:

Printed in the United States of America

Messages **From The Mercy Seat** is a collection of meditations born from time in the presence of the Lord, words of encouragement drawn from studying the scriptures, and gleanings from the sermons and sharings in our congregation, Global Truth Ministries. Hopefully it will strengthen your conscious knowledge of the righteousness that Y'hoshua (Jesus) purchased for you on the cross. It is designed to be one additional source of the sort of truth that renews the mind and brings you further into the fullness of your holiness. I hope you not only enjoy them but that they lift up your heart to the Lord.

PROLOGUE

What might stand out when you read the account of the building of the Tabernacle of Moses in Exodus, is that the first piece of "furniture" was the Mercy Seat. The place where Yahweh's presence settled in the Tabernacle was the starting point of the entire structure. The Mercy Seat resided in the last room, the Holy of Holies. In other words the whole thing was built from the inside-out.

Much more than just an architectural fact, it may say a lot about how our relationship with the Lord should be. All things with the Lord also begin from the "inside-out". That means that if we want things to manifest in our lives they must first be present within us-our heart, mind, and soul. It's a lot like what John said about our prosperity and health. (*Beloved, I wish above all things that thou mayest prosper and be in health, even as thy soul prospereth. -3 John 1:2*) If there were a central theme to these messages then it would certainly be this concept.

If you want things around you to change, let the Lord change the things in you, first. If there is trouble around you, let the Prince of Peace calm the storms within you. Let His Spirit rise within you and you will rise above every challenge that comes your way. Manifest his presence in your life from the "inside-out".

CONTENTS

Encouraging Yourself In the Lord ◈ 7

Seizing Righteousness ◈ 51

Times And Seasons ◈ 95

Power In The Promises ◈ 137

Part I

ENCOURAGING YOURSELF IN THE LORD

I f we lend strength and support to one another as we work out our salvation, then we begin to function as a body. Hopefully each of our struggles lends strength to one another and points us back to the Spirit and the Word as our source of encouragement. I once heard a preacher say that there are no strong Christians but there is a strong Christ, which enables us to stand in faith after we do everything we know to do.

Mercy Seat Message #1
"Encourage Yourself In The Lord"

In 1 Samuel 30, David and his army returned from battle to find their homes burnt to the ground and their families taken captive by the Amalekites. In the midst of his distress David managed to encourage <u>himself</u> in the Lord in order to know what God wanted him to do about the situation. To encourage means to put on strength, to stimulate your spiritual sensibilities about the steadfast love of the Lord.

When David then sought the Lord he did not immediately make a "request". He did not say, "Lord, return our wives and children to us." Instead he asked the Lord a question: "What do you want me to do about this? Should I go after them and overtake them?" To David's presumed relief, the Lord told him to go after them and he would recover everything.

So often when distressful situations arise we don't take the important step of encouraging ourselves first. The spirit of God lives "in us". When trouble comes we need to first seek that which lies within, rather than just throw our hands up and hope the Lord will do something. He has already done something. He has given you the Holy Ghost to lead and guide you.

Once you have encouraged yourself, ask Him what <u>He</u> wants, not just what <u>you</u> want. Be assured that whatever He says it will all turn out for blessing, even if it does not go the way your request would have suggested. When you encourage yourself in the Lord you are not only able to hear his directions better, but the prayers and support of others begin to have real meaning, as they confirm and edify that which you have heard from the Lord. Without encouraging yourself, the best efforts of family and friends provide only temporary relief from your fears and anxieties. Encourage yourself in the Lord. He is "in there" waiting to give you what you need to go on.

Mercy Seat Message #2
"To Guide You Into All Truth..."

We have been given the Holy Ghost, said Jesus to "...guide us into all truth." (John 16:13) What does it mean to be guided into all truth and what are the implications for believers? For one, to be guided means that the Holy Ghost "leads the way" for us in our fulfilling the will of God for our lives. His primary tool in leading the way is his ability to "teach" us through the word of God that has been planted in our hearts and minds.

He teaches us the "truth", to deal with "reality from God's point of view" rather than our human perspective. Sounds pretty obvious, yes, but consider the implication. There is no need for an arduous effort in trying to figure out what to do with our lives in the grand scheme of things because we are being "guided". We hardly ever even have to question the situations we find ourselves confronting because, unless they are the product of unrepented sin, they have been put before us for us to learn something important to our fulfilling his will.

Continuing along this line of thinking should cause all of us to relax...stop trying to figure everything out.... enjoy the moment... seize the time...and trust that our "tour guide" knows the way. Understanding this will cause you to perhaps see your entire existence in a new way: you are not passing through time....time is passing through you.

Mercy Seat Message #3
"Your 'Metron'"

In Ephesians 4:7 Paul says that each one of us is given grace according to the measure (metron) of the gift of Christ. The word 'metron' means a predetermined, moderate amount and it refers to the application of the gift of Christ that we have been given in order to complete the work that he saved us to do.

While there are lots of aspects to this scripture the critical notion may be your understanding that you have a definite, specific, and personal role in God's plan for redeeming all creation. You were not saved at random along with a bunch of other folks. No, God in his infinite wisdom (and in my case, at least, a real sense of humor) saw how your personality, demeanor, experience and make up could be an asset to his plan and saved you in order to equip you to occupy your 'metron'.

The knowledge that you are a purposeful creation should give rise to all sorts of awesome joy about who you are and give you resilience to the issues that life brings your way. A narrow-minded boss, devious co-worker, unappreciative spouse, or insensitive friends should in no way be able to do much damage to your sense of value. After all, you have been given a metron that no other human being on this planet now, before, or in future can fill. Don't that make ya' feel good?

Mercy Seat Message #4
"The Power of Praise"

On a Sunday morning praise comes easily. It's the rest of the week that can present a challenge, especially if you are also facing any sort of trial. The power of praise is that it provides "360-degree" benefits.

Upward- Psalms 181:1 tells us that heaven itself is a place of praise and when we join in with the angels and the heavenly host we are lifted in our spirits to sit with him in those heavenly places.

Downward-Psalms 42:5 speaks of the need to praise God even in the depths of our despair so that his countenance will look upon us. Praise can reach down into the depths of our darkness and shine the light of his glory.

Inward-Psalms 103 tells us to bless him with all that is within us. Praising God opens up the heart and soul to receive the love, strength, intent, and anointing of God in our lives.

Outward-We are reminded in Psalms 98:4 that his praise reaches the whole earth and as we lift up our voices to him we are releasing his joy, grace, and mercy to all around us.

So whatever state you find yourself in today find the courage to praise him. Nothing can stay the same when the spirit of the living God comes on the scene!

Mercy Seat Message #5
"Narrow-Minded Christians"

You may have already heard sources, like the media, refer to committed Christians as being "narrow-minded". In our culture today that is a serious indictment, that a person might not be open to ideas that are different from their own.

While the love that we have for all people enables us to show tolerance for others and their beliefs, being "narrow-minded" is actually a tremendous compliment if you consider the words of Jesus. He said... "wide is gate and broad is the way that leads to destruction and many there be that go in thereat. But strait is the gate and narrow is the way that leads to life, and few there be that even find it."

As Christians we have intentionally chosen the "narrow way". There are thoughts, behaviors, ideas, concepts, and values that are destructive to spiritual life. We have to make intelligent decisions about what to allow into our frame of reference. We have to screen out that which is evil and cling to that which is good. We are called to cast down vain imaginations and anything that exalts itself against the knowledge of God.

To think that all ideas and approaches are equally beneficial is foolish. Be tolerant? Yes, absolutely. Accept everything as valuable and healthy? Not hardly. The next time you hear us referred to as narrow-minded think of the words of Jesus and rejoice.

In the Revelation, John was told to write to the church of Ephesus- "Nevertheless I have somewhat against thee, because thou hast left thy first love. Remember therefore from whence thou art fallen, and repent, and do the first works; or else I will come unto thee quickly, and will remove thy candlestick out of his place, except thou repent."

Keep your "loves" in order. Keep Jesus first.

Mercy Seat Message #6
"The Secret Place"

It's likely at some point during the day or week you will find the need to "get away." The pace, the demands, the pressures ...can all lead us to the need for some space. As believers we are fortunate to have a place we can always go. Psalms 91:1 tells us, "He that dwelleth in the secret place of the most high shall abide under the shadow of the almighty". This secret place is a place of devotion, of defense, and of deliverance.

We can enter into this secret place-the very presence of God himself-just to worship him. To let him know how thankful we are for this life now, and for that which is to come. You can stand in his presence without fear or shame and hear him tell you of his great love toward you and his intentions of blessing and keeping you.

If the enemy is warring against you, you can go into his presence as if it were a high tower and find safety. The secret place is where no demon in hell would dare enter, where trouble cannot find you. It is a place where you can dwell under the shadow of his wings.

When the battle rages beyond your faith to stand against the enemy, go to that secret place. Just as he told Moses as he and the children of Israel were backed up against the Red Sea: "The Lord will fight for you and you will hold your peace."(Ex. 14:14)

So whether it is for devotion, defense, or deliverance, "come boldly to the throne room of grace to receive mercy and help in a time of need."

Mercy Seat Message #7
"The Value of A Vision"

Do you feel sometimes that your life lacks meaning? Is your daily work boring, dull, and emotionally-draining? Grab the bigger vision God has for you and you will gain a new zeal for everything around you.

If you work for an organization there's a good chance that you've heard about the efforts to establish a 'vision' as part of the planning process, for example. Whether they use the concept properly or not they are, for the most part, on the right track. Having a vision is a very valuable thing for an organization or an individual.

What's your vision? That is, are you sensitive enough to the spirit of the Lord to know his purpose(s) for your life? How does he intend to use your uniqueness to impact the world for Jesus the Christ? What need has he planted on your heart that for you to fulfill would truly make your life "worthwhile"?

The prophet Habakkuk tells us to "make the vision plain upon tables (a 'billboard' in our language) so that he who sees it would run with it when he reads it." What he is telling us is that comprehending even a small part of the Lord's vision for your life will touch your heart in such a profound, energizing way that it can become the motivator for getting up each day, working hard, and applying yourself diligently to what is put before you...with joy!

Mercy Seat Message #8
"The Need for Discipline"

We all know that we are 'disciples' of the Lord Jesus Christ. To be a disciple literally means a "disciplined follower". So while the world often scoffs at the idea of discipline, we as believers know the value and importance of embracing a disciplined lifestyle. That discipline, according to Webster's is the "training that develops self-control...acceptance of, or submission to authority."

First, we know that we must discipline our "will". Ephesians 6 speaks to "doing the will of God from the heart". We routinely find ourselves in our own personal Gethsemane where we choose His will over our own, even when we would rather not.

We need to discipline our "ways". Our old nature as suggested by Isaiah is not inclined to follow His paths. The Lord says through the prophet that "your ways are not my ways. Your thoughts are not my thoughts". But as born-again believers we submit our ways to God and allow him to lead us in paths of righteousness for His names' sake. In doing so our new nature receives the priority.

Our "words" also need to be brought under the control of the Holy Spirit. The power of life and death are in the tongue as Proverbs tells us. We should be disciplined to choose life when we speak forth.

Finally our "work" must be disciplined. Don't be one of those deluded saints who doesn't think the Lord wants them to work for the kingdom of God. We have to set aside our personal goals, ambitions, and careers to be available for the cause of Christ.

If you allow the Lord to discipline your will, your way, your words, and your work, you will witness a wondrous walk.

Mercy Seat Message #9
"The Prayer of Jabez"

You have probably run across the inspiring message about Jabez in 1 Chronicles. This chapter contains the lengthy genealogy of the 12 Israelite tribes. In Chapter 4 Jabez is introduced and has an incredible distinction in the brief description of his life.

In addition, his petition before the Lord is included, "Oh that thou would bless me indeed, and enlarge my coast, and that your hand might be with me, and that you would keep me from evil, that it may not grieve me! And God granted him that which he requested."

Many of us have found that this short passage to be an inspiration and an encouragement to seek the Lord's blessings even more and to believe Him for the best things. We are learning to ask the to 'bless us indeed' is not selfish. Try it, you'll like it!

Mercy Seat Message #10
"You Can M-O-V-E Mountains"

Jesus says in Matthew 17:20, "If ye have faith as a grain of mustard seed, ye shall say unto this mountain, Remove hence to yonder place; and it shall remove; and nothing shall be impossible unto you."

I'm sure we would all like to have "mountain-moving" faith. In fact, it's not that difficult to believe God for the seemingly impossible, if we understand how to apply ourselves to the Word of God.

First we must be MOTIVATED. If you really do hunger and thirst after righteousness God will fill you with a knowledge of himself that causes you to agree that all things really are possible with him.

Second, we must walk in OBEDIENCE. How is it that we continually rationalize our disobedience, somehow thinking it will be overlooked? Amazing huh? If we do walk in obedience however, we will be equally amazed at how fast and how powerfully we "activate" the law of the spirit of life.

The third aspect of mountain-moving faith is VISION. Literally this means that we need to see the finished work of God before us. Remember that "faith is the substance of things hoped for...the evidence of things not seen."

Finally it takes ENDURANCE. Do you really believe that the principalities and powers will easily give up their territory? Do you think they will readily give way to your manifesting the awesomeness of God, which would cause others to believe also? Of course not. To move mountains we must be able to wait and hang in there. Remember you already have the victory.

So keep on praying, keep on believing and wait for the Lord's timing. Jesus said that believing faith could do the impossible. You really can move mountains.

Mercy Seat Message #11
"In the World..."

In John 17 Jesus' prayer to the Father says that although we are in the world we are not of the world. As the attraction of our culture grows stronger we must make a concerted effort as individuals and as the body of Christ to be the "church".

The "church" has never been a congregation or even a building where people meet. The word 'church' is the Greek word 'ekklesia' which literally means "called out". We are called out of the darkness of sin to the light of glorious liberty in Christ. We are called out the bondage of death to eternal life in the presence of Almighty God. We are called out of worthlessness as common flesh and blood, to be the righteousness of God in Christ Jesus. We are called out of the mediocrity of this culture to a life of supernatural love, joy, peace, longsuffering, gentleness, goodness, faith, meekness, and temperance.

As Esau sold his birthright for a bowl of porridge, we must not sell our birthright as citizens of a heavenly kingdom. Do not let your everyday occupation or professional capacity take away from you your honored position as an ambassador for Christ.

Mercy Seat Message #12
"Ears to Hear"

We are co-laborers with Christ and the Lord is waiting patiently on some of us to do some labor! Having ears to hear means that we have developed a sensitivity to what the Spirit of God is saying and doing and have the unction to walk out our role in His plan. The fulfillment of all of those marvelous scriptures ("I can do all things...", or "My God shall supply...") comes in the process of our taking a step of faith to do what He has called us to do.

We all get in a "slump" from time to time. But it is critical to seek the Lord for the energy and enthusiasm to do the work of the ministry. Simply believing is not enough. Remember that "faith without works is dead".

The fields are white unto harvest. Come join the laborers in advancing the kingdom of God. Have ears to hear and act on what he is telling you to do. The time draws near.

Mercy Seat Message #13
"A Relationship With the Lord"

I really enjoy the beach. The pounding surf reminds me of where the Bible says that God's voice is like the sound of many waters. The burning brightness of the sun and the blowing breeze seem to elevate my spiritual senses. On my last visit I learned something about relating to the Lord.

Initially, driving by the beach, I could smell the salty air and gaze at the endless horizon but that was not enough to really experience it. Soon after, as I sat there in the sand it was better, but from a distance it was still not enough. Something in me longed to be more a part of it so I plunged into the water and rode a few waves. Though fun, I was still not involved the way I wanted to be (and it felt a little like work). Finally I took my chair and plunked it down right in the surf. As the tide came in, the water periodically covered me and I stayed there for hours, listening to the roar of those many waters. It reminded me of the Lord, and how to have a relationship with Him.

What did I learn, you say? We can all gaze at him from a distance and know of his power. We can even be near him or work to feel his touch. It is only when we take a seat in the midst of his presence that we truly can hear his voice and know that He is God.

Mercy Seat Message #14
"Depend on the Lord"

Picture yourself hanging onto the branch of a tree with your body dangling over the heights of a dangerous cliff. How does it feel? Can you sense the tightness of your grip on the branch and your tremendous hope that it will sustain you as you dangle?

The word "depend" literally means to "hang down". I know the Lord is a "firm foundation" and that we are to "stand" when we have done all we know to do according to Ephesians 6. The other aspect of our reliance on God is to "depend" on him. To see the importance of holding onto him minute by minute and to feel the sustaining power of the Holy Ghost in our every waking moment.

The wonderful difference with the Lord is that the fear you would experience holding on to that branch does not exist. Rather than the horrifying expanse of empty air underneath you, there is His guiding hand to support you as you "hang down." Rather than the "hope" that the branch will sustain you, there is the evidence of faith in knowing that He is the one who is "able to keep you from falling."

Mercy Seat Message #15
"Which Way Do I Go?"

We are all regularly in need of direction on our lives. Daily decisions, tough circumstances, and moral choices confront us continually. The key to success is knowing that the Lord has already made a way for you, and then finding that way. When you are facing the need for direction here is some wisdom from Psalms 25 on how to receive it from the inside of your being.

1. **"Show Me"**- Psalms 25:4 says "Show me your ways O Lord." God shows us His way in His Word, in prayer, meditation, and praise. When we acknowledge His control of our situation it says in Proverbs 3:6 that he will then direct our paths.
2. **"Teach Me"**-Psalms 25:4 also says, "Teach me your paths". If you are set in your own ways you will find it hard to make good decisions. If you are willing to surrender to the Holy Ghost He will, as it says in John 14, "teach you all things." Being teachable allows to easily receive God's guidance.
3. **"Lead Me"**-Psalms 25:5 pleads for the Lord to "Lead me in your truth." If you are not seeking the truth, all of your decisions will end up costing you. If you deal with truth, even the worst of circumstances will yield a blessing to you.

Mercy Seat Message #16
"The Main Thing"

A street-wise philosopher once gave this advice about life. He said that the "main thing is to keep the main thing the main thing...". Though not intended to be a tongue twister, it does offer some insight into our walk in the Kingdom of God.

Jesus, in Matthew 28, gave us the only instructions we have for what we are to do. We are to 'make disciples'. In simple terms it means to lead, guide, and nurture others as "disciplined followers" of the Lord Jesus Christ. While there are lots of other things we do around that 'main thing', we must be careful to always ask ourselves how our actions are contributing towards that goal.

If we can answer this confidently on that Great Day, then we have an assurance that His words to us will be 'well done thou good and faithful servant'. The main thing is to keep the main thing the main thing.

Mercy Seat Message #17
"God's Sovereignty"

When those of us who are saved bowed our knee to the Lord Jesus Christ we accepted the free gift of His eternal righteousness in exchange for the mortal wretchedness of our own lives. In accepting this gift we agreed with Him that our life was no longer ours but His.

Our culture would have us believe that we have something to say about God's presence in schools, or street corners or in any arena of public life. Our society suggests that his reign can be limited and legislated to those venues where it is deemed acceptable.

What a sad and fearful surprise it will be for all when He reveals our folly in the last day. He is sovereign and the bounds of His rule cannot be dictated. He is king over all and his dominion cannot be measured or contained. This is a message we are tasked with sharing with those around us for as Isaiah says He will make a swift end of things when He closes the books on this age. Share this truth and save a life.

Mercy Seat Message #18
"What Are You Looking For?"

From the beginning of Jesus' earthly ministry, and even after His bodily resurrection, the children of Israel were expecting a very different kind of Messiah. They were looking for an earthly king that would free them from the control of Rome.

What kind of Messiah are you looking for? Is Jesus just the source of your deliverance from the temporary trials and circumstances of life, or is He your commanding officer as you take your place in the army of the Lord? Are you looking for Jesus just to supply your thirst for possessions and material things or are you seeking first the Kingdom of God and His righteousness, believing He will add all these other things to you? Who are you looking for?

Much of the body of Christ is still anticipating that Christians will rise to power and transform society by the impact of our system of morality. While that may happen, much of the scriptures say that we are simply to occupy and declare the Kingdom until He returns. On that great day when the Lord returns with a shout, whom will you be looking for?

Mercy Seat Message #19
"Communing With the Lord"

The act of remembering Jesus by partaking of the Lord's Supper can be the most meaningful experience a believer can have or it can become just a meaningless ritual. The depth of love symbolized in this act of remembrance is worth meditating on. In the bread we see Christ freeing us from the dominion of sin. The Bible tells us He joyfully endured all aspects of the breaking of His body in anticipation of His communion with us as future sons of God. As He shed His precious blood, the wine we partake of reminds us that God has taken His sacrifice as payment for all of our sins, past, present, and future.

The next chance you get to share in the Lord's Supper...take your time. Ponder the love that this sacrament (meaning 'sacred') represents. Do it as often as you will in remembrance of His great love for you.

Mercy Seat Message #20
"The Authority of God"

The first several verses of Romans 13 tell us that all authority originates with God and that we are to put ('subject') ourselves under God's arrangement of that authority. That means that your supervisor or boss is put there by God and your subjection to that authority is a place of blessing for you. (I can hear you saying," yes, but you don't know my boss!")

Just as David obeyed God's choice of an undesirable Saul as his authority, so may you be facing the same circumstance. And just as David's possessing of his kingship was dependent upon him handling the situation in a Godly manner, so does yours.

"Pray for those in authority", the Word tells us, because if they are a godly authority He will enlarge their capacity to bless you. If they are an ungodly authority your obedience will produce even more blessing for you in the midst of the circumstance. And the Lord will change the hearts of those who would be your enemy.

Mercy Seat Message #21
"Can He Trust You?"

I often feel as if the Lord is looking to see whom he can trust with His authority in the earth. The key to being trusted is found in Psalms 1, which tells us to neither walk, stand, nor sit in a place of evil.

Maintaining the righteousness that was credited to our account by the blood of Jesus equips us to exercise God's authority in our lives, with the right heart attitude and purity of motivation.

You and I need that authority. To do the Lord's will, even to simply go about our daily duties, we need to possess the highest level of God's power we can since we have an enemy who seeks to take our lives. Allow Him to make you trustworthy and see His glory shine through you.

Mercy Seat Message #22
"Living Epistles"

The Book of the Revelation proclaims that one day the tabernacle of God will be with men. This could mean that we will be the dwelling place of His fullness in an even greater measure than the infilling of His spirit has made us now.

Paul calls us "living epistles" and as you and I grow closer to the Lord, our very presence lights the darkness around us. As we grow up into the fullness of the likeness of His stature, our very presence, like Peter's shadow, brings healing to a hurting humanity.

Continue to grow. Continue to hunger and thirst after righteousness. He wants to manifest His life through yours.

Mercy Seat Message #23
"A Way of Escape"

The Bible tells us that with every trial or temptation the Lord makes for us a way of escape. Often we assume that this means that He will divinely alter the circumstances or remove us from them.

When Jesus was at Gethsemane, just before He was taken to be crucified He asked the Father to "take this cup from me." In other words it seems like he was asking the Father to "remove the situation I am facing." But then He added, "but not my will be done...". Jesus seems to have been asking that if the situation cannot change, then 'change me in the situation', cause me to accept your choice knowing it must be the best for me even if it doesn't seem so.'

Quite often God's way of escape for us in our trials is to change the way we see and understand the trial. Rather than remove the burden He sometimes simply gives us the shoulders to bear it with joy. He then reminds us that all things are truly working together for our good.

Mercy Seat Message #24
"Problems With Purpose"

In Chapter 5 of the Book of Romans Paul says that he 'glories' in tribulation. This meant that he had learned to greet the pressures of life's challenges with an attitude of 'joyful boasting', happy to be facing such circumstances.

Paul certainly wasn't the glutton for punishment that it may seem. No, it's just that he had enough experience with God to know that each challenge brought with it a greater abundance of blessing. The patience ('cheerful endurance') that was produced by these challenges was based upon Paul understanding that a loving God always has a divine purpose when we are faced with trials.

No matter what comes your way today, whether by God's choice or your own doing, know that your willingness to take faith in the Lord's ability to deliver you will produce great blessings. Remember that with the Lord, every problem has a purpose.

Mercy Seat Message #25
"Let Your Light Shine"

It's a shame that we have limited 'ministry' to being behind a pulpit or to be one endowed with a "title". In doing so we risk belittling the power of each believer to be used by the Lord as a powerful instrument of righteousness.

Obviously the Lord has ordained some folks to be apostles, prophets, evangelists, and pastor-teachers...people with specific functions. But those of us who are sitting in a cubicle today, behind a glass partition, or leaning on a backyard fence, all carry an equally powerful anointing to be those 'living epistles'.

If the Lord calls upon you today to speak a word to someone-do it. But if all He asks of you is just to do your work with diligent service, do it well. People around are peering through the darkness to see how you will behave and respond to the pressures and problems of the day. If all the Lord asks of you is to minister His influence to the spiritual darkness around you, just by being there... let your light shine.

Mercy Seat Message #26
"Today If You Hear His Voice..."

In Psalms 95 we are admonished to hear God 's voice and obey it, much the same as sheep respond to their shepherd. Sheep are by nature skittish and frightful. A close, "personal" relationship with the shepherd is essential for their survival. The sheep know the shepherd by his voice and the shepherd knows each sheep by name.

They follow him on their daily journey from one location to the next. At the watering hole, when it is time to depart, he simply calls out their names and his sheep will follow him to their next stop. They will refuse to follow any of the other shepherds who are also calling out the names of their sheep. When he calls they will respond immediately because they have learned that their lives will depend on obedience to the shepherd.

They have watched the shepherd defend them against wolves and other predators. They know that the Valley of the Shadow is much scarier when they are out of contact with the shepherd. Sound familiar? Well then, today if you hear his voice, harden not your heart".

Mercy Seat Message #27
"A Kingdom of Priests"

In Exodus 19 the Lord tells the Israelites that if they will obey his voice and keep his covenant, among other things, he would make them a "kingdom of priests".

We normally associate priests with those with the special responsibility to represent people before the Lord. In the Old Testament the required gifts and sacrifices were brought to them to present to the Lord. They were set apart for this work and the Lord provided for all of their needs.

While you and I may need apostles, prophets, evangelists, pastors-teachers to edify us as the body of Christ, we don't need anyone else to go to the Lord on our behalf. He wants to establish a personal relationship with you and I as we come before him. Put on your robes of righteousness, wash yourself with the water of the word, and enter in.

Mercy Seat Message #28
"Faith Without Works"

While we know that we are not saved by good works we often forget the role that works play in the ongoing process of salvation. James 2 tells us that we demonstrate our faith by works. In other words, the proof of our salvation is exemplified by the actions we take.

You may have noticed a startling distinction between people who are receiving the joy of their salvation and those who never seem to experience the boundless freedom of a life in Christ. Those who are always giving to, and doing for others, seem to rise above every circumstance. Those who focus mainly on their own issues crumple in the face of the slightest obstacles.

Faith without actions of love towards others produces "death", a decay and atrophy of the soul. Faith with good works initiates the law of sowing and reaping, whereby the Lord even causes others to give back to you such blessings that you cannot even contain them.

Mercy Seat Message #29
"Patience With The Process"

The hallmark of salvation is the hunger and thirst for "seeking the Kingdom of God and His righteousness". Those people who are simply content with just 'going to heaven' have missed the opportunity and responsibility to grow in grace and in holiness before God. Salvation begins at accepting Jesus as Lord and Savior and continues as we submit to the perfecting power of His will for our lives.

It's easy though to get out of balance. In our zeal to submit to sanctification and the renewing of our minds, we can grow impatient, becoming critical of ourselves and the 'progress' we are making. It's good to demand more of yourself but not more than He is demanding of you.

He truly has begun a good work in you and He will complete it. Chances are, if you are walking in repentance and adhering to God's law, you are probably right where He wants you to be. Be patient with the process. You've got forever.

Mercy Seat Message #30
"Despise Not Small Things"

God called the prophet Zechariah around 520 B.C. to encourage those who were rebuilding Jerusalem after the Israelite's release from captivity. The Lord says through the prophet "... who would despise the day of small things?" He prophesied that their eyes be opened to see that they were a part of much bigger building project than they could imagine.

It was hard for those who had spent years in bondage to gauge the magnitude of their task. They could not see that every brick they added to the walls that surrounded Jerusalem, and each piece of the temple they restored, was putting creation that much close to the return of the promised Messiah. They could not see they were part of building God's eternal kingdom.

You may be behind a desk, a lawnmower, or a group of excited children today. You may be tempted to see your circumstance as small beginnings. You may want to question whether you are doing anything useful with yourself. Do not despise the day of small things. Your life, your work, even the monotonous errands you will run can have divine significance. Just ask the Lord to open your eyes.

Mercy Seat Message #31
"Broken Bread"

If you don't stay focused it's easy to momentarily 'forget' why the Lord saved you. Our culture encourages people to pay so much attention to 'self' that we can become confused about the terms of the covenant that we entered into. Upon accepting Jesus as Lord and Savior, we gave up control of our lives. We agreed to submit to his purpose for our lives above our own desires.

When Jesus took the five loaves, broke them and fed the multitudes, he may have also been saying something to us about those purposes. The disciples gave him their sustenance, which he broke, and supplied the needs of others with that sustenance. There was so much left over that the baskets could not hold it.

Get the picture? Jesus is working in your life to make you a whole 'loaf' so he can break that bread to feed others. Don't worry, it doesn't hurt, and what will be returned to you in blessings will be more than you can hold. As I said, we are told that the person who tries to hang on to his life will "lose" it, but "losing" your life to the Lord is the guarantee that you will find it. When the Lord says 'pass the bread, please,' just let go off the loaf.

Mercy Seat Message #32
"Power To Be Witnesses"

In Acts 1:8 Jesus tells the disciples that when they receive the Holy Ghost they will get power to be "witnesses". The word witness is the word we know in English as 'martyr'. And, in fact, much of the growth of the early church came from unbelievers observing the incredible peace and serenity of Christians as they were slain for their faith in the Lord.

While in some parts of the world today there is martyrdom occurring, at least for now, we in the United States have enjoyed the freedom to spread the gospel without fear of death. There is, however, an important application for us as well. There are co-workers; neighbors and relatives who are watching our witness to the Lord to see if we too have 'died'.

They are watching to see if we have died to material possessions, to pride, and to the lustful appetites that they knew we were once drawn to. They are watching to see how real Jesus is by how much we have decreased and how much He has increased in us. The most powerful evangelism may not be your ability to quote Romans 10:9-10. The most powerful witness to them may just be the evidence of your changed life.

Mercy Seat Message #33
"Staying Put"

Knowing the will of God for your life can be challenging at times, but often it is just a matter of doing what He has told you do...until He tells you to do something else. As easy as that may seem, you and I both know it can be difficult to execute.

As salt and light, His will may be for us to be put in the most inconvenient or untenable circumstances. For example, many of us are in work places where we may as well have 'Saul' as a supervisor. Others may be faced with significant health issues for season, where all the prayer and repentance have failed to deliver us. Still others find themselves in relationships that seem to yield little value, but we can't get released from them.

David did have Saul for a supervisor. Although he too probably wanted to get out of the situation, the Lord would only tell him to 'stay put'. Because of his obedience, David learned the very lessons he would need to carry out God's will for his life as King of Israel. Wherever you find yourself today, if you have discerned it is the Lord's will for you, then stay put. Know for certain there are lessons to be learned and a crown to be obtained.

Mercy Seat Message #34
"All Honor"

We sing a worship song in our Sunday services with the lyrics "...all honor, all glory, all power to You." The word 'honor' implies an <u>action</u> that we take towards God, not just an <u>attitude</u> of reverence.

'Honor' literally meant to pay tribute or to give an offering in recognition of the greatness of the one being honored. Because of the blood of Jesus there is no price to pay, only the offering of a life submitted to do His will.

Honor Him by first, thinking godly thoughts...forgiving others, blessing others, being used by the Lord as an instrument of peace. Then do. Honor the Lord by making a sacrifice to help those in need, especially someone you know that doesn't really deserve it.

Mercy Seat Message #35
"Like A Refiner's Fire"

In Malachi 3 the Lord is said to be like a refiner's fire and a purifier of silver. The image is a powerful description of how He brings forth the character of Christ in us.

The silversmith places the unrefined metal in the middle of the heat to burn off fits impurities. He cannot be casual about his work, as keeping the silver in the flames a moment too long will destroy it. As Malachi says, he "sits" gently holding it and watching the purification process take place. Once the smith can see his own image in the silver he knows it is ready.

When we endure situations and circumstances, our natural reaction is often to moan, groan, cry, and complain. At some point, however, we need to respond to the Lord's dealings with us. We need to let Him see His image in us. And when He sees it, the flames die down and the precious metal is ready for the Master's use.

Mercy Seat Message #36
"He Who Endures To The End..."

In three of the Gospels Jesus describes what the end of the age will be like. He concludes each by telling us that he who "endures to the end will be saved."

While we commonly think of enduring as putting up with difficult circumstances, it actually means to 'stay under' or 'stay behind'. Jesus could have been saying that in the time of the end he who stays under... His grace, His mercy, in obedience, in submission to His will and His word...will be saved. The implication may be that he who stays behind... and follows the path that the Lord is leading him in....will be saved.

Nothing counts more than our personal relationship with the Lord. No amount of church attendance (though good), no amount of giving (though needed), and no amount of good works (though blessed), can replace the constancy of that personal relationship. He who stays under the shelter of His wings will always be saved.

Mercy Seat Message #37
"Assembling Ourselves Together"

Paul admonishes the Hebrews in chapter 10 not to forsake the assembling together as the body of Christ. He is naturally referring to the Christian worship service, but his words mean far more than an encouragement just to attend church.

The word 'assemble' means to have a 'complete collection'. Just like when the parts of a car are 'assembled' it has to be a complete collection for the automobile to run well, if at all. As the body of Christ, we also represent a completion collection as every member of the body has a function and role that no one else can perform.

Encourage yourself to do more than just attend. Find your role and apply yourself to it, so that your church will function as that complete collection. Prepare your heart to receive the word of God through the music, the preaching and the teaching. Before you enter into that place, be ready to assemble yourselves, not to just occupy a place on a pew.

Mercy Seat Message #38
"A Prisoner of the Lord"

In Ephesians 3 the apostle Paul refers to himself as a "prisoner of the Lord for the Gentiles". More than just a servant, he has relinquished control of his life and ministry.

The analogy of being a prisoner of God should fit for all of us as believers. Prisoners have no say in what they do and when they will do it. They have no choice in whether they will follow the directions of those who guard them. Likewise we should follow the Lord's direction without choice and, go where He tells us to go, to do what He has called us to do.

The big difference is that a prisoner in society is in a place of punishment for wrongdoing. He or she has committed a crime for which justice must be served. Paul, as a prisoner of the Lord, was in a place of blessing to be an instrument of mercy. Let us go and be likewise.

Mercy Seat Message #39
"One Body"

We need to be reminded of the power of the oneness of the Body of Christ. As it says in 1 Corinthians 12, the church has many members, but they all make up just one body. It is in the diversity of that Body that God manifests Himself.

Often our natural minds resist the concept of diversity. We can tend to feel more comfortable when people and their giftings are more like our own. Unfortunately, what can be most comfortable is not necessarily more anointed. If Proverbs is true, and 'iron sharpens iron', then we need to embrace the diversity of the Body of Christ.

In your own congregation, everyone, in one way or another is 'different'. It is only when you function together, that each difference finds its unique niche and its opportunity to make the whole better.

Mercy Seat Message #40
"The Day of Judgment"

Peter tells us that God has fixed a day when He will judge the actions and intentions of the wicked. The Lord has preserved the ungodly for that time when they will stand before the Him and have the 'Book' of their lives opened and examined. The certainty of this event has been verified by Jesus' resurrection from the dead, according to Acts 17:30-31.

Regardless of your particular eschatology, this fact should give you an even greater level of commitment to share the Good News to those around you. It should impress on our heart an enhanced sense of urgency to live our lives as an example of the compassion of Christ.

We are told that we are God's epistles, living letters to be read by friends, family, and co-workers who need to see the light. Ask the Lord today to increase His work in you so that your light would shine for all to see. Give the unsaved around you the chance to be spared from God's judgment on that Great Day.

Mercy Seat Message #41
"Denying Yourself"

In Mark 8:34 Jesus says that "...Whosoever will come after me, let him deny himself, and take up his cross, and follow me." To many, this phrase may suggest a life devoid of even the most basic of life's enjoyments or the possession of material things. While we are to stay free from the lusts of the flesh, this verse says much more than any of that about following after Him.

To "deny yourself" refers to abandoning your self-interest, of no longer being preoccupied with that which you feel is important. Instead we are to allow the Spirit of God to establish within us, that which is important to fulfilling His purpose for us.

The blessing of taking up the cross is the "crucifixion" of those desires and goals, which are not a part of God's plan for you. Instead He will resurrect within you a hunger to see His will worked out in your life. In exchange He will multiply back to you all that you need, and more. Funny, isn't it? Denying yourself is the key to receiving God's abundance.

Mercy Seat Message #42
"Rejoicing In Hope"

Romans 15:13 tells says that...*"the God of hope fill you with all joy and peace in believing, that ye may abound in hope, through the power of the Holy Ghost".*

We often find ourselves in challenging circumstances where we need to have our hearts filled with hope. The scriptures seem to suggest that hope is built on faith, produced by joy and rejoicing. To rejoice is to literally <u>put yourself</u> in a sound frame of mind. In other words, our ability to experience hope is first born out of our 'knowing' that the challenge is under the control of God's sovereignty.

He will never let you down. Remind yourself of all of the many times that He has kept His word to you. This will give you the ability to rejoice. If you can rejoice then your faith will rise up and produce hope in your heart.

Mercy Seat Message #43
"On Guard"

Psalms 19:11-14 in part mentions "... cleanse thou me from secret faults." It is these "secret faults" for which we need to be on guard. As believers, we know the error of blatant and premeditated transgressions. And since the devil knows we know, it is less likely that he will attempt to lure us into such gross neglect of the Lord's commands.

It is in the 'secret sins", the yielding to gossip, the tolerance for apathy towards spiritual things, murmuring against the boss, or the failure to shine our light when darkness creeps in, where we are often the most vulnerable.

Be on guard today. Know that sometimes the 'roaring lion' as Satan is referred to, can purr like a kitten, seducing you to slack up in your vigilance against his trickery. Be on guard today at the seductiveness of secret sins.

Mercy Seat Message #44
"Back To Basics"

Never overlook the importance of sticking to the basics of the word of God. The "fear of the Lord is *(still)* the beginning of wisdom." No matter what we know or how we grow, we will always need to soak ourselves in the scriptures so that wisdom will dwell in us.

Although the depth of spiritual things is to be sought after, the basics of putting the word in you will never change. We are still to feed on that sincere milk of the word that we would grow. God's word still changes you on the inside first, and then it shows up in your outward behavior and attitude. In all of your goings, His word will continue to be a "lamp unto your feet and a light unto your path".

I would encourage you to never abandon the things that caused you to learn more of the Lord's goodness-reading, memorizing, cherishing, and obeying the simple truths in the scriptures. Life may get complex, complicated, and convoluted but the Kingdom of God will always be simple and straightforward *if* you stay in the word.

Mercy Seat Message #45
"Not Your House!"

In Malachi, the Lord tells us the reason for being obedient to the tithe principle and to giving offerings. He says that it is important that there be "...meat in My house...". While we often rightly think of tithing and giving offerings as the way to insure that our needs our met, we often neglect the underlying theme.

I would maintain that scripture has multiple levels of meaning. Tithing is one of those examples. Among the several reasons is that we tithe as a response to God in replenishing creation with that which we took away to produce the increase itself. In turn He is "obligated" (best word I could come up with), if you will, to take care of us. If His house is "full", therein lies the abundance by which your barns become full and your presses overflow with new wine.

The Levites (the Old Testament order of Priests) were not permitted to toil to take care of themselves, as a portion of the tithe was used to meet their needs. As Peter said, we are that priesthood that God seeks. In turn, He will take care of us. Tithe and give offerings, not so your house will be full, but that the Lord's blessings will be on your house. Then, He will surely fill it.

Mercy Seat Message #46
"Through The Fog"

The Lord is always teaching and confirming His word to us. On a recent car trip I encountered intense fog which made it impossible to see but only a few feet ahead. While I wanted to go the normal speed limit I had to go more slowly to reach my destination.

Every now and then a more adventurous traveler would whiz by, tempting my impatience to follow after them at full speed. It occurred to me, however, that we might both end up in trouble if I trusted that person's ability to see! And so, I settled into the tenuous task of limping along in the mist.

It all reminded me of our walk with Him. Many times our human limitations can cause us to become frustrated and lose patience when we cannot see clearly on the road He has us traveling. We are often motivated to trust in other people, as our frustration with not going faster grows. Ultimately though, as Isaiah says, "..precept by precept, line upon line, line upon line, here are a little, and there a little.." is the best way to make it home.

Mercy Seat Message #47
"God's Love Toward Us"

We all know that God loves us. What's sometimes difficult to comprehend is the depth of that love. It is so unlike any love we have known from other human beings.

First of all, His love is the self-sacrificing kind. There are many parents who would give up their lives to save their child. There are probably none who would give the life of their child to save a total stranger. Especially one whose conduct and habits make them totally undeserving of being saved to begin with. Selah.

God's love towards us is also without condition. As much as other people attempt to love us "no matter what", we are all afflicted with the subtle tendency to dispense greater measures of our love towards others when they 'perform' as we think they ought. God chooses to demonstrate His love for you knowing you neither deserve it, nor may not always honor it. That's a love that can be hard to comprehend. But it is a love that is real.

Mercy Seat Message #48
"Made As One Flesh"

At the end of a marriage ceremony it is customary to quote Matthew 5:19 to solidify the understanding of the covenant that is being created. "...What therefore God hath joined together, let not man put asunder."

This joining together was first established in the garden in Genesis when the Woman was pulled forth from the Man, becoming "bone of my bone and flesh of my flesh". In order to maintain that togetherness a husband and wife must work together with the Lord to make the best use of the ways in which they are different. Marital bliss is only achieved when each treats the other as their own flesh.

We have a number of single women in our church who are exceptional examples of being married to the Lord. In the same way as married folks, those of you who are single have the same responsibility. Jesus is whom you are married to, and He requires the same adjustments of you, so that you would conform to His image and do the things that are pleasing to Him. Whether single or married, we are all in a one-flesh ministry unto the Lord.

Mercy Seat Message #49
"Headship"

Our culture tends to look at leadership (headship) as being the one who tells everyone else what to do. In lots of marriages for example, the husband being the "head of the wife" can create lots of conflict if they lack a Biblical understanding of what it should mean. In the workplace we have lots of people who are managers or supervisors who create more ill will rather than creating a more productive work environment.

Jesus made it clear in Matthew 20:25-28- "...Ye know that the princes of the Gentiles exercise dominion over them, and they that are great exercise authority upon them. But it shall not be so among you: but whosoever will be great among you, let him be your minister; And whosoever will be chief among you, let him be your servant: Even as the Son of man came not to be ministered unto, but to minister, and to give his life a ransom for many."

Being the "head" means to set an example for others to follow. It's easy to tell others what to do when you have shown them... either by example or attitude, or both. Try it out. At work, at home, in the church.

Mercy Seat Message #50
"Be Silent"

Paul's words to Timothy about women keeping silent in church has been misused and misapplied for ages. Not to mention overlooked if you're into the "letter of the law". A good understanding of the purpose for Paul's letter and the events taking place in the Ephesian church help this scripture to be understood.

Ephesus was overrun by numerous "other gospels" many of which were versions of Gnosticism. Paul had warned Timothy not to let false teachers confuse people with these heresies. Many Gnostic teachers were women owing to the fundamental precepts of the errant philosophy. Paul welcomed the heretics (who were also believers) but forbid them to teach. They were to sit and learn so they could understand the truth of the 'real' gospel.

Throughout church history the failure to adequately understand the context of scripture has put all sorts of people into bondage. We are never to accept the surface explanation of even the most well-meaning expositor. We are to be, as Paul encouraged, like the Bereans who searched out the scriptures so the truth of God's word would be comprehended.

Mercy Seat Message #51
"No Complaints"

When the children of Israel ventured forth from Egypt through the wilderness they were heading to the land of promise that had been prophesied for generations. Unfortunately their Egyptian mentality followed them, turning what scholars tell us could have been an 11-day trip into a 40-year sojourn.

Part of the problem was their insistence on murmuring and complaining whenever things didn't seem to go the way they thought they should go. Whether it was the taste of the food, the threat of no water, or the fear of people they did not know, they constantly tried God's patience. Eventually all of those who were considered adults, died in the wilderness except for Joshua and Caleb. Their 'can-do' attitude saved them.

Things often don't go the way we want or expect. Following God is often not easy, but we have to trust His judgment even when the way is not clear. Whining, complaining, and murmuring will never get you to that place of blessing. It may even cause you to "die" in the wilderness. Making your complaints known to the Lord is a good thing as long you end the conversation by asking Him to change your heart and to cause you to want what He wants.

Mercy Seat Message #52
"Loving the Lord"

As believers we all know that we love the Lord. That love is a deep abiding knowledge of the goodness of God that should humble you when you think about it. But love is more than feeling. Love is an action and your "love" for the Lord should express itself as l-o-v-e that Lifts, Obeys, is Victorious, and Endless.

Your love for the Lord should lift others. It is a love that spills out over the confines of your own life and has an impact on the lives of others. In fact the more 'unlovable' a person may be, the more your love should penetrate their hearts.

Your love for the Lord should produce obedience in your walk with God. When you really ponder what God has done, is doing, and will continue to do for you, it will overwhelm you to the point that it should hurt to disobey him. The true gospel says that he will use grace to move you to clean up your act, not fear of his wrath.

Your love for the Lord is the source of victory in every aspect of your life. Knowing that 'no weapon formed against you will prosper' is a tremendous asset. Remember, it doesn't say that weapons won't be formed against you-it's just that they will not prosper!

Finally, your love for the Lord is endless. It is eternal. It should make every trial on this earth so temporary that you can the always see his grace in the midst. Endless love allows you to live your life based on your future and not on your past.

Mercy Seat Message #53
"Hard To Stumble"

One common theme in the scriptures is the importance if humility. In fact, James even says to humble yourself and the Lord will lift you up. Jesus talked about talking the lowly place at the banquet, and then being invited up to a more prestigious spot. The founding pastor of our church, Cameron Simmons, instilled in us the understanding that 'the way *up* with the Lord is *down*.'

To live, work, walk, and worship in humility is a precious and powerful thing. The dominant theme in our culture these days seems to be demanding "respect" from people. Prideful, arrogant, spiteful attitudes can ruin the choir, the men's group, and any ministry in the church where people are not wiling to submit to the Lord, through submitting to one another. Great marriages, however, are based on humility, on preferring your spouse above yourself and your needs. Great ministry is based on prayer, being humble before the Lord, bowing down on bended knees.

It is hard to stumble when you are on your knees. The opportunity for the enemy to disrupt, confound and confuse becomes increasingly more limited, the lower you get to the 'floor'. Even more important, is for your heart to be on its 'knees'. Dismissing prideful thoughts and distancing yourself from conceit and jealousy will keep you flowing in his grace.

Mercy Seat Message #54
"Faith, Hope and Love"

Without faith we cannot please God, for faith in Christ is being sure of what we hope for and certain of what we don't see. Through faith we know that God exists and that He will reward us as we earnestly seek Him. God often allows problems in our lives to strengthen our ability to depend upon him. Therefore, we consider it pure joy when we face trials because we know that the test of our faith develops perseverance. And perseverance develops character, and character produces hope, and hope does not disappoint us.

Ultimately, hope is that expectation of the return of Jesus to set up His kingdom and put things right. With hope we can meet the problems of today for we know that tomorrow will bring glory with Jesus. Therefore, hope makes it possible for us to rejoice in our sufferings. When our lives rest on a foundation of hope, we are able to give thanks to God and praise Him regardless of what happens. For we know that all things will work together for our good as God uses us to bring honor and glory to His name .

Our actions reveal how much love is operating in our lives. Love always protects, always trusts, always hopes, always perseveres and never fails. The reason our love will not fail is because of our hope, which is based on Christ being near us and causing all things to come out right.

So, with an active faith, hope and love we can meet the storms and sorrows of life and be victorious over the cares of this world.

If we have faith, hope and love working together we can love our enemies, bless those who curse us, and do good to those who persecute us. Then our joy will be so great that it cannot be expressed in words and our reward beyond comprehension.

Mercy Seat Message #55
"He Is Our Peace"

Philippians 4:7 refers to the "peace of God that passeth understanding." Perhaps no other commodity is more valued in our fast-paced, often stressful world, as peace. The absence of conflict and chaos is a prized possession. People will go to great lengths to do whatever they need to do, often those things that are ultimately destructive, in order to calm the raging storm in their hearts and minds.

For us as believers the problem is the same but the solution is quite different. We don't need any external stimulus or device to provide us with this cherished peace. In fact, the concept that there is an external stimulus or device that can provide peace, is an illusion in and of itself. Peace only exists in the presence of God. Any fleshy approach to obtaining it is fruitless, because there is no peace to be found "out there". Since God lives in us so does peace.

Learn to resist the temptation to look somewhere else when you need peace. Instead, learn how to calm your fears and feelings just long enough to reach within your own spirit and release the peace that dwells therein. Sometimes you might have to be like David in the Psalms and pour heart out to the Lord first. The Lord can handle your anger, frustration, and hopelessness. He can listen to you rant, rave, whine, and whimper. He has no problem with your problems. In fact He welcomes the opportunity to help you get it out of your system, then giving Him the opportunity to calm the storm. He wants the opportunity to be your peace.

Mercy Seat Message #56
"Worshipping God"

Matthew 4:10 says that"..*Then saith Jesus unto him, Get thee hence, Satan: for it is written, Thou shalt worship the Lord thy God, and him only shalt thou serve.*" The worship of God is much more than just the exuberance in our hearts when we sing songs of praise. True worship is our daily (evenly hourly) focus on our relationship with the Lord, and our obedience to his direction in our lives.

Lots of things can hinder this true worship. Allowing doubt and unbelief to dominate our thoughts will stifle our worship. Letting bitterness and unforgiveness fester in our souls will corrupt our ability to enter into the fullness of our relationship with him. Permitting the stain of sin to remain, without seeking God's mercy through repentance, will cripple our access to the throne room of grace.

You have to be determined in your focus on the things of God. Just like any "skill" it is important, if you will, to "practice" his presence and renew those areas of your mind that lack proper focus. Know, that God is at work to remove the blinders from your spiritual eyes, so that you can see the glory of his grace more clearly every moment, of every hour of every day.

Mercy Seat Message #57
"To Obey Is Better Than Sacrifices"

In 1 Samuel 15, King Saul is severely admonished by the prophet Samuel for failing to wipe out all of the Amalekites, as well as all that belonged to them. Saul had thought he had done a good thing by bringing the Lord a trophy of the victory. Unfortunately all of his good deeds meant little in the face of his failure to obey the voice of the Lord and do what he was told to do.

Unfortunately we can all find ourselves in the same boat. Although we may do many things that we believe are pleasing to the Lord, nothing quite compares to obeying the things He has told us to do. For example, to write the biggest check imaginable to support the work of a ministry bears little resemblance to forgiving the person who offended you last year, whom you still bear a grudge against. Yeah, giving the offering is great, but the only way that blessing will flow your way is through obedience.

Do not allow yourself to be deceived. God demands obedience and nothing can substitute for it. Thankfully there is mercy and grace to cover us as we grow in our ability to submit to His will. But ultimately it will always come back to doing what He has told you to do. As Samuel told Saul in verse 22 "...And Samuel said, Hath the LORD as great delight in burnt offerings and sacrifices, as in obeying the voice of the LORD? Behold, to obey is better than sacrifice, and to hearken than the fat of rams."

Mercy Seat Message #58
"The Force Of Joy"

Our culture advocates the quest for happiness and none of us would probably argue that it's a good thing to be happy. But "happy" has its limitations. The sense of elation and delight when circumstances are favorable can fade just as quickly as it came when things turn sour. Most often, our happiness can rise and set many times, even in the course of a single day.

Joy is different. As described in the scriptures, joy is the spiritual capacity to maintain a lighter heart and a more positive attitude than even the direst of circumstances deserves. Joy is the Lord's, and as a believer that force can operate in us and through us despite what may be happening around us. This capacity equips us to control how we react to things even though we can seldom control the things themselves.

You may need such 'force' even as you read this. If you are walled in by circumstances, or walled out by obstacles and problems, let the joy of the Lord that resides in your spirit, come to the surface and chase away the roadblocks. Let the assurance that His grace really is sufficient, enable and empower you to press on to victory, no matter the nature of the battle.

Mercy Seat Message #59
"A New Creature"

In 2 Corinthians 5:17-18 Paul tells us that"... *Therefore if any man be in Christ, he is a new creature: old things are passed away; behold, all things are become new. And all things are of God, who hath reconciled us to himself by Jesus Christ, and hath given to us the ministry of reconciliation;"*. To some this is an inspiring and encouraging scripture. To others it is life-changing revelation.

To be "new" does <u>not</u> mean to be repaired, or fixed up to a point where you are now tolerable in the sight of God! No, to be "new" literally means that God has created something in you that did not exist before, that which is 'unprecedented' on the planet. In this newness all that which was a part of the old person that was limited, incapable and inglorious, has been completely replaced. The new creation can do all things through the Christ which strengthens it.

We have to act, behave, and believe like new creatures in order to be new creatures. Refuse to let the limitations of your past dissuade you from doing that which God has been beckoning you to do. Refuse to allow any sense of inadequacy, guilt or shame for who were, to interfere with your perception of who you are now, as God sees you. Choose to not let sin direct and control your desire to live a life of holiness. This new creature is no longer a slave to sin. The new you was created free.

Mercy Seat Message #60
"Maintaining Our Focus"

Since our church has recently moved to a new but temporary location, we have immediately begun to seek the Lord for His direction for a permanent building. Last Sunday as we thought to initiate the normal Building Fund drive, the Lord gave us a word that caused us to rethink our priorities a bit.

During the Middle Ages the great cathedrals were built as a way of letting the world know that God was still present in the earth and that the gospel was alive. Often today, we build buildings that only further insulate us from those lost in sin, and so we only associate with other believers.

Jesus only gave the church one thing to focus on. It is found in Matthew 28:19 where we are told to go and make disciples. While buildings are nice of course and necessary as a place to congregate, we have to be careful not to let those aspects of the church distract us from that main focus. If we make enough disciples, the Lord will certainly have to help us find a place to put them all.

Mercy Seat Message #61
"The Power Of The Holy Ghost"

In Acts 1 Jesus (in his resurrected being by the way!) tells the disciples to wait together and they will receive power to become witnesses. Remember the word "witness" is the same word from which we derive "martyr", one who lays their life down in support of a cause. While believers are still being martyred in many places in the world, there is a level of meaning here that applies to all of us, whether we endure physical persecution or not.

Perhaps the most difficult aspect of being a disciple is when our will conflicts with God's will. At that crossroad we must make a decision to either abandon what we want and follow Him, or hang on to our own desires, knowing full-well it probably isn't the best plan. This death to self---our wants and perceived needs--- requires a power, the power of the Holy Ghost to be a witness.

Today, and everyday, you and I will face these kinds of choices, in both major life issues and the so-called "small stuff". To Christ nothing is small stuff or even major issues. They are all opportunities to seize the power of the Holy Ghost within us and make the choice that will bless God, thereby blessing ourselves abundantly. Wait on Him as He told the 120 in the upper room. Before you think or talk or act, wait. You will receive power from on high and if you let Him be who He is through you, you will be a wonderful witness.

Mercy Seat Message #62
"The Be-Attitudes"

In John 3:13 Jesus said "And no man hath ascended up to heaven, but he that came down from heaven, even the Son of man which is in heaven." No one but Jesus has the experience of having dwelt in heaven and no one but Him knows how to bring the quality of heaven down to earth.

Throughout the Gospels Jesus conveys to us the understanding of how we can accomplish this ourselves, in line with God's will for us. It is not our intelligence, strength, possessions, capabilities or talents that will produce blessings. It is the qualities of meekness, peace-making, and a hunger and thirst for righteousness that will produce heavenly blessings in our earthly existence.

Surely you want those blessings in your life. Surely you want heaven to come down in the midst of your 'earth'. What it will take is for your attitude and behavior to resemble Jesus'. He did not operate on the earth as God, but as a man who demonstrated what could be accomplished by a life without sin and that can apprehend the power of God through their character. Your blessings are yours for the taking. All you need are the right attitudes.

Mercy Seat Message #63
"Honor Your Mother And Father....
Even When It Hurts"

The fifth commandment carries an important promise. It says that if you will honor your father and mother you will live a long time upon the earth. You probably know someone who had a tough time in his or her childhood. They were not blessed with Godly, loving parents and they still show the effects of either direct or indirect abuse. These scars can run deep and cover up a lot of pain. It is a difficult issue to approach when you suggest that they should still honor their mother and father. Nonetheless it is God's desire for them and he adds a significant blessing to it whether their parents are still living or not.

To forgive does not imply to forget. It simply means that you have decided not to pay the person back who hurt you, by harboring ill will towards them in your heart and mind. No one can forget what has happened to him or her, but the Lord wants to be the one to repay those who have wronged you, rather than have you do it. Honoring an undeserving mother or father does just that, it removes the need to get back at them for their shortcomings and failures as a parent. It will also do wonders for you.

Having a long life is not just about the amount of time. It also refers to the quality of that time. Much of the productive capacity of someone who is harboring understandably-bad feelings towards their parents is lost in the quicksand of unforgiveness. The ability to release the power and creativity God has planted in you can be crippled by the inability to forgive and continue to honor them. Thus an already bruised heart is wounded yet again. If you know someone who is suffering this all-too-common agony, share with him or her the restoration power of a Mighty God. Let them know that God cares deeply for their pain and has offered a solution. It is perhaps the opposite of what worldly wisdom would suggest but it works, every time.

Mercy Seat Message #64
"Built Upon Sand"

Mathew 7: 24-27 says....." *24* Therefore whosoever heareth these sayings of mine, and doeth them, I will liken him unto a wise man, which built his house upon a rock: *25* And the rain descended, and the floods came, and the winds blew, and beat upon that house; and it fell not: for it was founded upon a rock. *26 And every one that heareth these sayings of mine, and doeth them not, shall be likened unto a foolish man, which built his house upon the sand: 27 And the rain descended, and the floods came, and the winds blew, and beat upon that house; and it fell: and great was the fall of it."*

Jesus' "sayings" represent the truth of the Old Testament and its fulfillment and realization in the New Testament. It is the importance of our singular focus and obedience to God, and our application of His truth in our conduct with one another. Too often in the church we create varied definitions of what God wants from us, ranging from regular attendance on Sundays to praying a certain number of hours. Obviously all of those things are good. We should be in church and we should definitely pray. The point is however; will these things alone cause our house to be built upon a rock?

Jesus makes it clear, it seems, that the foundation of your house needs to be His "sayings". The foundation needs to be a dedication to reading, studying, and incorporating the Word. Take note that this does not include listening to the teaching of someone else that has read and studied and incorporated the Word. It is incumbent on each of us to "put in our own work". To do so guarantees a house that will withstand the storms of life. To ignore this truth runs the risk of living a house that one day may fall.

Mercy Seat Message #65
"Thou Shalt Not Steal"

You would think that this commandment was one those spiritual 'no brainers'-an obvious issue that should be pretty easy to avoid. When you also think about things like the reluctance to tithe and the failure to be generous with offerings, other definitions and explanations begin to hit home. People steal because they do not know God, or do not trust God, even if they know Him. Most of you reading this probably fall into the latter half of the sentence. We make decisions to hang on to what actually belongs to God (tithes) or to the person(s) He is directing that our money be used to help (offerings).

Even bigger issues entered our minds-things that we all need to pray about. Elected officials who "steal" the trust of the people and then disappoint them with unethical behavior. Dictators and rulers who "steal" the freedom that God intended for people to enjoy. Greedy corporations who rob the air and water of its God-given vitality. We've got a lot to do, you and I, to help restore back to the all creation what sin has stolen.

Mercy Seat Message #66
"Thou Shalt Not Covet"

In Exodus 20:17 coveting includes the desire for something and the sequence of manipulation that it takes to get it. In many cases these actions are actually "legal" in and of themselves, but are being woven into a fabric of deception. In the Old Testament the teachings of Moses were first to be applied to the "nation" and then to individual households and people.

Some areas of our nation can be insidiously covetous. For example, many contracts in business are filled with clauses in the fine print that can cause an unwary participant to be defrauded. Government dealings can smell of collusion with those who would profit from laws that protect the privileged at the expense of the poor and less educated. We must always be mindful to pray for those in authority that their thoughts and actions would honor the law of God.

Naturally as individuals we must, as it says in Colossians, "mortify our members", so that we are not given to errors such as covetousness. Playing office politics to get the position you want, or manipulating your spouse to satisfy your personal desires, are all dangerous games. They are likened to "idolatry" because; rather than allow the Lord to direct the outcomes in our lives, we choose to orchestrate our own results.

Mercy Seat Message #67
"Light Afflictions"

2 Corinthians 4:15-17 reads like this" *For all things are for your sakes, that the abundant grace might through the thanksgiving of many redound to the glory of God. For which cause we faint not; but though our outward man perish, yet the inward man is renewed day by day. For our light affliction, which is but for a moment, worketh for us a far more exceeding and eternal weight of glory;...".* These "light" afflictions? Are you kidding me?

No, not kidding at all. While you and I sometimes feel the burden of our trials and tribulations, in the eyes of God, they <u>are</u>

small things. Small, because He reckons that we have taken the notion of Jesus living His life through us literally. Thus to God, any earthly burden must by definition be a light one. But perhaps the most important reason for why these are light afflictions is found in the last verse.

Everything we suffer in this realm of reality makes a contribution towards the apprehension of the full measure of God's glory. In other words, these light afflictions will eventually give way to heavy rewards. These temporary ills are fertilizing that which will spring up for your eternal joy. The things that try to keep you down are the very things that God causes you stand on top of for eternal blessings. Keep your head up. Trouble will come to pass. It will <u>not</u> come to stay.

Mercy Seat Message #68
"Honor Your Father And Mother- Again"

Every child who has spent any time in church has heard the fifth commandment. They have been taught that it is their duty before God to respect, obey, and follow the guidance of their parents so that their days will be long. The commandment did not need to emphasize the duty of parents to be honorable, that was a given, in a community governed by God's law. Unfortunately we are not in that situation today and find ourselves with an increasing difficulty in raising children that will honor their parents. Some of it is due to the effects of our culture on the young ones. Much of it is also an increasing number of parents who are not honorable.

Naturally this does remove the obligation of honoring from the children. It just makes it that much more difficult. Parents who do not respect truth, who do not understand the need to set the proper example, who are too young or too selfish to be parents... all affect the way that children see God. If a parent does not present the right image of godliness, it will be very hard for a child to see it anywhere. When that child becomes an adult they may have a great deal of trouble in relating to the character, mature, patterns and principles of God.

We all need to have a heart for parents in these days. It has always been a tough job and has only gotten tougher. Parents need love, support, truth, and encouragement to make sure they are being the kind of people that can be easily honored. Whether at work, in the neighborhood or even inside your own family, look for ways to be a source of strength for a parent who is struggling to do what is right in the eyes of God so that God will be seen through them in the eyes of their children.

Mercy Seat Message #69
"Losing Your Life"

Jesus said that he who seeks his life will lose it and whoever loses his life for the sake of following after the Lord will find it. I'm sure there are numerous correct interpretations of this passage. One thing that occurs is the pressure we sometimes feel to "figure out" what the Lord wants for our vocation, ministry, job or career. "Losing your life" may well mean giving up the need to try to so closely control the outcome.

Naturally we should make plans and seek Godly wisdom in moving through the maze of opportunities set before us. But while we are moving, we should remind ourselves that the Lord is moving too. He is steadily going ahead of us to prepare the way for His will to come to pass in our lives.

So relax. Lose your life. Resist the temptation to fret and worry over the next step you need to take. Begin to praise Him for His plan for you and ask that your eyes be opened to see it. Go ahead, lose your life and then find it. Find the joy, peace, contentment, and prosperity He has ordained for you.

Part II

SEIZING RIGHTEOUSNESS

O f all the lessons the Holy Ghost has taught me the most powerful is the vital need to fully and completely grasp our righteousness. If you don't "know" in the depths of your being that the price paid on the cross was sufficient then you'll never really believe that you deserve to be blessed. You'll say the right things but their manifestation will be retarded because you really live in a state of guilt. You were not only freed from the penalty of your sin nature but also from the consciousness that you even once had a sin nature. Study Romans 8:1-3 and look up the meaning of the words!

Mercy Seat Message #70
"By Grace We Are Saved Through Faith"

Yeah, I know, I know, you understand that it is not by works that we obtain salvation, but through faith in Jesus the Christ. And I'm sure when you first accepted the atoning work of the cross you knew you could not earn it. But what about now?

How often today will you cringe at an ugly thought of yours or even the thoughtless ugliness that can suddenly erupt from an otherwise holy heart? Will you wonder if the Lord will "smite" you for your wickedness? Will you concede the loss of a blessing or the receipt of a curse because you messed up? Will you decide to do something good to make up for your mess?

If you were saved initially through faith in the blood of the lamb you are continually being saved by that same faith. Cringing at ugliness is good as long as it leads you back to the confession of your need for that blood. If faith saved the wretched thing you were when you first came to him, how much more will faith in Him save you today?

Mercy Seat Message #71
"Whose Point Of View?"

Ephesians 2 tells us that in salvation we were raised up together and caused to sit together in the heavenly places in Christ Jesus. Because of God's grace, and for no other reason, we were freed from the bondage of a sinful nature. Even when we were still held captive by that nature, and often enjoying the pleasures of that nature, God chose to extend his grace towards us.

That clearly means that we had no real hand in deserving the great gift of that grace. Nothing we could have done, or can do, will earn it. According to the scriptures, God' point of view is that because of the sacrifice made on the cross, we have been made worthy of righteousness. His point of view does not change based on how we feel about ourselves. We would do well to adopt His point of view.

Seeing ourselves as unworthy of grace simply makes it easier to allow sin in our lives. We subtly can excuse ourselves from allowing Christ's perfection to rule our decisions because, subconsciously, we have already accepted failure based on what we are. However, seeing ourselves as the scriptures say <u>God</u> sees us encourages the resistance of sinful impulses. We now unconsciously accept power over sin based on who he is. And consciously, our awe at God's boundless love for us overwhelms the need to any longer consider sin an option.

Mercy Seat Message #72
The Lord Is "With" You

At the end of the sixth chapter of Joshua there is a profound statement. It says that the Lord was "with" Joshua. We know that Joshua fought many battles to lead Israel through the Promised Land. He was victorious roughly 95% of the time (his record was something like 31-1-1) because the Lord was "with" him.

It's one thing in the battles that we fight to know that God is there. But if we don't grasp the fullness of his presence, our minds will tell us that he has just come by to watch us struggle and hopefully to glorify him if we somehow manage to win. The truth however, the glorious truth, is that he is "with" you. He is not a spectator in your struggles but an active participant arming, equipping, and encouraging you to seize the already-won victory. And if the conflict rages beyond your capacity or your faith to believe, he will himself take up the fight for you.

By the way, Joshua's lone defeat came as the result of sin in the camp of Israel. Our margin of victory increases as we walk in the righteousness of God that Jesus has made us to be. Know today that God is not only for you. He is "with" you.

Mercy Seat Message #73
"Repentance-A Change of Mind"

Repentance is a lot like visiting the dentist—you don't necessarily enjoy it but you know it's really important. What happens a lot with repenting is that we fail to get the full benefit. After all, God gave it to us as a way to insure blessings in our life despite our tendency to disobey. The more you see it as an opportunity, and not the punishment for messing up, the better you will get at it. Although you're probably real sorry for whatever you did, repentance is not about being sorry. The sorrow <u>leads</u> to repentance but feeling bad is not the point. The word means to "think again". In other words we are asking God to help us think differently about the situation or issue that led us to disobedience.

If we think differently about it then our actions toward it will change. For example, if your sin is that you eat too much (ouch!!) and God causes cherry pie to be as a plate of mud to you, you'd begin to stop craving it. (Hopefully :) The Holy Spirit is at work in us to help the renewing of our minds, and repentance is the channel through which much of that renewing can take place. Embrace repentance. Get good at it. When you mess up ask the Lord to help change your mind about the issue. You will never really be free of a sin until you die to the need that it satisfies.

Mercy Seat Message #74
"Being A Confident Christian"

Philippians 4:13 says that "I can do all things through Christ which strengthens me." How often are we challenged to make this scripture real in our lives and reach for something to help us bring it to light? There are 4 "P's" that you might find helpful in 'doing all things'. There first is **"Positiveness"** To do all things you must think you *can* do all things and tell yourself that it is possible if Christ is strengthening you. So often we defeat ourselves by saying "I can't" even before we have given Christ a chance to work through us.

Second is **"Performance"**. If we are lazy, fearful, or unconcerned we will not walk through the door that God opens. Often we must walk through one door to have others opened. As James warned be not a hearer only. (NEVER THINK THOUGH THAT PERFORMING IS RELATED TO BEING MADE RIGHTEOUS-THAT'S DANGEROUS TO YOU.)

Next is the **Person**. Remember that if God has called you to a work or allowed a challenge to come into your life he is "obligated" to equip, enable, and encourage you to complete it as he works through you.

Finally there is **Power**. With the equipping through the person of Jesus the Christ comes the accumulation of power in your life, a reservoir of the power of the Holy Ghost that wells up in you like rivers of living water.

Of ourselves we are nothing. But if you act in faith, assured that Christ is working through you, you cannot fail.

Mercy Seat Message #75
"Draw Near to God"

James tells us to "Draw nigh to God and he will draw nigh unto you." If you're like me you might often get it backwards. We wait for God to somehow increase his presence with us to encourage us to draw near to him. It's not that he won't make the first move-he has-he put his Holy Ghost in us as a constant presence. For us to 'activate', if you will, what is in us, we need to take some steps.

First there is prayer. Prayer creates the communion that allows us to sense the presence of God. Sometimes this means quiet time and real concentration to avoid the usual distractions around us.

Next we need to search the scriptures to uncover the promises that God has made to us. These promises assure us of his willingness to meet our needs. Thus we draw even closer to him.

Finally we can sing his praises. The Bible tells us that he inhabits the praises of his people. Praise will release you from yourself and give you the unction to draw close to him.

And the next thing you know is that you are engulfed in the glory and peace of God. All cares, trials, and problems melt into the light of his being. All fear is replaced with the wonder of his love.

Mercy Seat Message #76
"Whose Point of View?"

The concept of being "made righteous" in the sight of God by the work of Jesus on the cross is the most profound fact that a Christian can embrace. It means a number of different things, all leading to the conclusion that our own point of view about ourselves, other people, etc., can be largely irrelevant.

For example, when problems arise it is far too easy to become mired in the cares and succumb to worry and fear. The Bible tells us that we are seated in heavenly places in Christ Jesus. (Ephesians 2:6) Grasping this as a fact rather than just a metaphor enables us to 'look down' on our difficulties realizing, at worst, they are only for the moment.

Understanding the concept of righteousness is critical also in maintaining the proper sense of self. While the world preaches the doctrine of "self" esteem, we find our esteem in the price Jesus paid for our salvation. That alone makes us precious and we do not have to fall into the trap of satisfying anyone else's image of who and what we should be.

The concept of righteousness completely and totally removes everything from our past selves that would be unpleasing to God. Even as we make mistakes in our walk with God he has extended forgiveness to us and will always see us as pure and holy as he sees Jesus himself. What an awesome thought!

As the forces of darkness try to encroach upon you remember to see things from God's point of view. We have been made perfect in his sight.

Mercy Seat Message #77
"Rules, Rigor or Relationship?"

The context of the New Testament outlines what seems to be a progression of our faith in Jesus Christ. First, upon accepting the gift of salvation we are "justified" ('made right') in the sight of the God. As the Lord works in our lives we are further "sanctified" ('made holy') by the work of His Spirit. Ultimately we will be "glorified" ('transformed into his image and likeness).

God's plan seems to be for us to appropriate this progression into our lives. Our understanding of this can have powerful consequences on the quality of our walk with the Lord.

For example, if we are only aware of the debt that was paid for us and live at the level of justification we will lapse into adhering to "rules" in order to perfect our walk with God. We will even unconsciously attend church, pray, read, or praise as requirements of drawing closer to him.

If we focus only on sanctification we may get locked into the "rigor" of working to overcome the imperfections that still plague our personalities. This means that, in effect, our past is still determining our future.

If we live rather on the basis of what is to come and develop an eternal perspective based on "relationship" to God, then our future determines our present. We can then live as the scriptures say in the "glorious light of liberty", knowing that we will be glorified when the King comes. We will then attend church, pray, read, or praise because we are drawing closer to Him.

There is no condemnation for living at any level of the kingdom of God. As the young people say' "it's all good". (We say rather that 'it's all God'.) The encouragement is to seek the very best and deepest "relationship" with Him. It is there you will find the rest that we all so desperately need.

Mercy Seat Message #78
"How To Increase In Love"

Since the greatest gift is love (1 Corinthians 13) we all would probably like to have more of it flowing through our lives. Here's a brief prescription that is guaranteed to work:

1. Think with love- Too many Christians dwell on the worst-case scenario instead of thinking on that which is "lovely". (Philippians 4:8) Filling your mind with loving thoughts towards yourself and others will cause love to abound toward you.
2. Listen with love- When we cry out to the Lord, he listens because he loves us. Jesus listened to the needs of those around him with an ear of love. If we hear the cry of others with an ear of judgment or criticism we will receive the same.

3. <u>Speak with love</u>- We know that a "soft answer turns away wrath" (Proverbs 15:1). We increase in love by using words of hope, faith, encouragement and understanding. The words we also say to "ourselves", in our own minds, should bear the same qualities as well.

4. <u>Labor with love</u>-When it's all said and done, love is really an action that we take. Putting your hands to work to express the love of God will cause that same love to be measured back to you.

The scriptures tell us that the world will know us by the love we have for one another. Let your light shine. Increase in love.

Mercy Seat Message #79
"Who Do You Say That He Is?"

In Matthew 16:13, Jesus asked his disciples, "Who do people say that I am?" The answers they gave included John the Baptist, Elijah, Jeremiah, and one of prophets of old (Matthew 16:14). By this time, John the Baptist was dead, killed by Herod Agrippa, the ruler of Galilee (Matthew 14:1-12). Which means that all the names offered to identify Jesus were the names of dead prophets, one of whom, they believed, had miraculously come back to life again.

In our thoughts and eventually in our conduct we answer this question everyday. Unfortunately we frequently come up with a different answer depending on the circumstances we are facing.

The Lord desires to strengthen each of us today in the knowledge that it is our decision to always be able to answer as Simon Peter did: "You are the Christ, the Son of the living God." Circumstances cannot defeat the Christ in you. The issues of life cannot weaken his anointing that has been conveyed to you. The insensitivity of others and even our own waywardness cannot dim the light of his glory that shines through us.

Lift up your heads, oh ye saints and be lifted up ye eternal creatures of God, for the King of glory has come in. Who is the King of glory? Jesus who lives in you, he is the King of glory.

Mercy Seat Message #80
"It's In the Details"

Ever heard the expression, "the devil is in the details"? As unedifying as it is, there may be a grain of truth in it. Those of us who really want to have a deeper and more intimate relationship with the Lord must be willing to turn over the smallest details of our lives in order to achieve that intimacy. After all, it's hard to become close to someone who we are not willing to share those secret places in our lives.

Secondly, the power of sin lies in the way we handle ourselves when we are all alone. It's easy to put on the right face and say the right words when all the saints are gathered around. When you're in the company of your own thoughts however, malice and wickedness can seep into the most trivial details of our minds and pollute that temple.

Is the devil in the details? Perhaps not. But it is in the details of our lives that we find the chance to give God his ultimate glory-the possession of our hearts as his throne.

Mercy Seat Message #81
"A New Way of Living"

We are told in the Epistle to the Romans that the "law of spirit of life in Christ Jesus has made us free from the law of sin and death." The essence of this scripture is that, as a saved person, you and I have been given the legal right to live life at a different level. We are no longer under the control of sin, darkness, and the fear of mortality. We are no longer in bondage to the urges and passions of the flesh. Our decisions cannot be controlled by our soulish desires and impulses.

No, you and I are empowered to invoke God's laws such as sowing and reaping, forgiveness, or blessing those that persecute us. Each of these principles brings forth a "death" of our selfish will and "resurrects the power and glory of God in our mortal flesh, as it says in Corinthians. Each time we participate this way in the "sufferings of Christ" the Lord multiplies his grace into our lives and brings forth greater light into the dark areas of our heart.

Not only can we rely on the promise of an eternal life with the Lord, but we can also possess the peace, joy, fullness, and victory of the life of God right now. Don't settle for the crumbs off of the table. Allow the Lord to change your will to his, operate in the law of the spirit of life, and take your seat at the banquet table.

Mercy Seat Message #82
"Fight For Your Rights"

The concept of salvation is full of subtleties that can sometimes confuse the natural mind-we give things away to receive, lose our life to find it, etc. Another important notion is that we must 'fight' to receive (or maintain) that which is already ours.

The Word is true when it says that we have been blessed with every spiritual blessing in heavenly places in Christ. At the same time, the forces of darkness, our own flesh, and the attraction of the world, are constantly at work to rob us of those same blessings. But we can only be robbed if we fail to yield to the authority of God's word and his Spirit.

To 'fight' in this sense means some very simple but powerfully effective things. (1) Renew your mind with the Word of God. Know what God says about you and what he has done for you. (2) When the accuser tries to bring guilt or shame upon you, call it the lie that it is and embrace God's favor, which is always extended towards you. (3) Stand in faith for the Spirit of God to rise up big within you.

The Kingdom of God suffers violence, as the Gospels say, and the violent take it by force.

Mercy Seat Message #83
"Righteousness Through Faith"

The scriptures tell us that we are the righteousness of God by Christ Jesus. That righteousness is appropriated through faith in the work of Jesus on the cross and in his bodily resurrection as the Son of God. "Faith" is a much talked about concept and in some circles has been turned into a tool that we try to use to get God to do things for us.

The true faith that produces God's perfection in our lives (his righteousness) does not come from formulas or scriptural 'incantations'. No, the righteousness-producing faith of the Bible comes from three factors:

1) A spiritual union with God gained from spending time with him and learning to rely on his faithfulness in all your life situations.
2) Obedience to God's will in your life, including doing what he has commanded you to do, as well as choosing to refrain from that which he has commanded you not to do.
3) A progressive transformation of your character and behavior towards the likeness of Jesus in the way you act and think.

Nothing else will produce the blessings of salvation. Don't let anyone fool you. Being the righteousness of God cannot be earned or achieved. It is given freely as an act of God's grace.

Mercy Seat Message #84
"Nailed to the Cross"

It's funny how often our mental image of what God is thinking about us, is so different from the reality of his thoughts. He never sees us in the depths of sin but from the pinnacle of his grace. In fact he will move to re-move the need that the sin was trying to satisfy.

From the moment of repentance, whatever sin we were committed to is "nailed to the cross". Meaning, it is covered by the blood of the crucified Christ to the point where the sin is no longer visible. It is we who can choose to retain the stain, the guilt, and shame of our wickedness. God has forgotten it.

Are you remembering your own sin right now? If so, why not take a moment while you are reading this and repent. Ask the Lord to change your mind about the sin you are committed to. Once you do, it is nailed to the cross. He will have already forgotten and your slate will be clean in your mind too.

Mercy Seat Message #85
"Hunger for Holiness"

It is sad, but it seems to be true, that our culture has accepted the fact that a life of holiness is a useless and unnecessary pursuit. Sin is seen as a natural consequence of being human and efforts to insist upon an adherence to God's expectations are viewed as "extreme".

What may be even sadder for Christians, who accept this point of view, is that the Lord does not, in fact, feel that way. Through the cross he has freed us from the need for sin and expects that we would make progress in divesting ourselves of sinful practices. While biologists and geneticists make excuses for our being "born that way", the Lord's notion is that we were all "born again" which negates the consequences of whatever our DNA may have wrought in us.

Today, ask the Lord for a hunger for holiness. Let the righteousness of God take over your thoughts and actions. The fear of the loss of familiar but deadly habits will soon be replaced by the boundless blessings of obedience.

Mercy Seat Message #86
"How Long Does It Take to 'Come Boldly'? /Too Good To Be True"

In broad terms, the concept of grace teaches us that the imputation of God's righteousness to our lives is a free gift that cannot be earned, deserved or repaid. We should definitely respond by good works and godly behavior, and God's intention is surely that the comprehension of the vastness of this love will lead us to holiness. But none of that will cause us to merit grace.

As easy to accept as this deal would seem to be, many of us still spend wasted time on guilt trips when we fall short. A good test of your comprehension of grace might be how long after making mistakes does it take you to "come boldly to the throne room of grace"?

While 'immediate' may be too soon (Godly sorrow does play a role in repentance), hours, days, or (God forbid), months or years, is wasted time. God's foreknowledge has already accounted for even tomorrow's evil. The shed blood of Jesus has already looked ahead and made provision for next week's transgression. So, "come boldly", and receive that mercy to help in times of need. As a my good friend Rev. Lynn Hiles says, ' if it's too good to be true, it's probably the gospel.

Mercy Seat Message #87
"An Angry God"

In the interest of making God acceptable to our culture much of the church would rather depict God as a benign and merciful being incapable of anything but love and goodness. While not totally incorrect for sure, even this image fails to illustrate the full measure of this goodness.

In reality God is incredibly angry. His wrath has seethed and brewed for ages at the rebellion and wickedness of man. His hatred of sin will be enough to cause him to eventually, according to his divine plan, destroy the curse of sin that has been levied. Now enters His love.

Rather than display this fury upon you and I for our sinfulness, He chose to direct his hostilities toward his Son and allow him to suffer the consequences of God's indignation towards us. Though you and I deserve the death that our sinfulness brings, God chose to 'be' the sacrifice in our place.

If you call yourself a God-fearing believer this should cause you to bow your knee to the Most High God in awesome recognition of his grace. It should cause you to obey, not out of the fear of an angry God, but out of the love of a God whose grace has spared you.

Mercy Seat Message #88
"Reverence the Lord"

To "reverence" means to exhibit a profound awe and respectful adoration. It's a wonderful thing that we are shedding the trappings of religion. It's good that we are emphasizing a personal relationship with God, rather than just going through a few solemn rituals. But you know, there is something to be said for the "solemn" aspect of experiencing the beauty of the Lord.

There are times, like in worship or in taking communion, where we need to exhibit the reverence, the profound awe and respectful adoration for God. In those times, the holiness of God and the glory of His presence should cause us to quiet ourselves, to ponder His infinite greatness, to sense him dwelling in us.

Reverence for the Lord will bless your life. The 'fear of the Lord is the beginning of wisdom" and respecting His awesome-ness will deepen the reservoir of that living water that flows in your life. Reverence the Lord. He is worthy to be adored .

Mercy Seat Message #89
"Enlarging the Circle"

Romans 13 is one of several places where we are told that "love fulfills all the requirements of God's Law". This love is a self-sacrificing, preferring-others-before-yourself, lay-down-your-life kind of love. But we are plainly told that the act of practicing this love is the complete fulfillment of God's holy expectations. What could be simpler?

I encourage you therefore to enlarge your circle of love. Ask the Lord to identify ways and people to whom you can show this love. I'm not talking about time-consuming complicated things. This world has grown so cold that even the smallest acts of love have a mammoth impact.

Practicing this love will enrich your life in ways beyond your wildest imagination because "blessed is he who delights in the Law of the Lord."

Mercy Seat Message #90
"No Middle Ground"

There is a subtle misconception in the world (and even among some in the church) that God's kingdom can be resisted. In Luke 10:8-11 Jesus tells the disciples essentially that whether people welcome the gospel or reject it the kingdom of God is still here.

Whether unsaved people accept the free gift of salvation or not, God's dominion will still direct their lives.

Whether you or I accept the commission to go out and make disciples or not, the age is still winding up and we will have to account for how we handled the gift we received.

Today is the day to shake off any complacency and the malaise of the culture that surrounds us. Today is the day to step out in the purpose for which you were saved. The kingdom of God is near you.

Mercy Seat Message #91
"The Choice of Humility"

We are told in Philippians 2 to have the same mind that was in Jesus. That "mind" was the decision to voluntarily and progressively humble himself in order to do the will of the One who sent Him.

Not only did Jesus choose to divest Himself of His rightful dignity as God, but he further lowered Himself to occupy a human body, though a sinless one. As if that was not enough, He debased himself further to experience human weakness and then even to endure the humiliation of dying like the worst sort of common criminal on a cross.

For those decisions he was highly exalted and given an identity to which all creation must acknowledge. Humble yourself in the sight of God today and he will exalt you too. Make the choice of humility.

Mercy Seat Message #92
"He Is Worthy"

At some point during the day you will be faced with a situation where the devil will try to convince you that you are not worthy....not worthy of God's answered prayer...not worthy of insight into a problem at work...not worthy of a promotion...not worthy of a peaceful household when you get home.

Rather than engage in a debate and try to work up the faith to believe, why not just agree? 'You're right, devil. I am not worthy of any of those good things that I want and need to come my way'. Agree, because the issue is not whether or not you are worthy. The issue is that He, the Lord, is worthy.

The Lord's blessings are yours today because he has chosen to bestow them on you based on the worthiness of the Christ. And because you are saved that worthiness has been charged to your account, just as your unworthiness was charged to Jesus' account as he hung there on the cross.

Mercy Seat Message #93
"Perfecting Those Things"

You and I know that the Lord has a purpose for us to fulfill in the earth. We know that he has called us to do his will and to perform some "earthly" actions that will possibly have eternal consequences in the lives of others. Knowing truth like this can have a paralyzing effect. 'What really is his will and how do I know I am doing it?'

Take heart to know that if we are obedient to take the first steps, even in uncertainty, doubt, or fear, he will complete the journey through us. If you will launch out the boat like Peter did, he will take your hand and cause you not to sink.

Even if you are a bit off base in your obedience, the fact that you have been willing to take those steps will be blessed. He will use your errors as an offering and multiply clear direction back to you. His promise is that he will "perfect those things that concern you."

Mercy Seat Message #94
"The Comforter"

Before Jesus ascended he promised the disciples he would not leave them comfortless, but would send to them another like Him in every way. That Comforter is obviously the Holy Ghost, given to every believer to lead and guide us into all the truth.

The Comforter also can comfort. He can speak to you today in the midst of a stressful workplace and remind you that he has gone ahead of you and prepared the way, no matter how disheartening things might look. He can remind you today that the lost son, wayward daughter, or estranged spouse can never beyond God's grasp, and though distant from you, they are all still reachable.

He can remind you that the Lord is a keeper of all the promises he makes and will honor that word spoken to you about the course of your life, even if today you can see nothing that resembles that promise. The Holy Ghost is the Comforter called to stay beside you and lead you in paths of righteousness for God's sake. And yours.

Mercy Seat Message #95
"Keeping the Law"

The New Testament makes it clear that we, as believers in the Lord Jesus Christ, are longer "under" the Law (for example, the Ten Commandments). That means that keeping the Law is no longer a condition for salvation, for we have received redemption by grace, through faith in the finished work of the cross.

The Law is still very relevant to us. It will always represent God's expectation for our behavior towards Him and towards others. The difference now is that we have been given the Holy Ghost, who through the work of sanctification enables us to live in obedience. No amount of effort, performance, or penitence will earn our position of righteousness.

Rather than feel condemnation for our shortcomings, we can have confidence that the Holy Ghost is continually leading and guiding us in the truth. The forgiveness found in the blood of Jesus being always available to us for those shortcomings as we walk out our salvation.

Mercy Seat Message #96
"By Faith Abraham..."

There are probably times when the things the Lord speaks to me are so far beyond my grasp that I wonder how it can possibly come to pass. There are instances where he compels me to go in a direction that I have never gone in before.

I've read that Abraham had the same experience. He was directed to leave his homeland and journey to a place he had never seen, nor even knew about. The destiny of all creation rested on his willingness to follow after God, trusting His word even though Abraham could not see the outcome.

Like Abraham you and I must overcome the doubts and fears that surround our hearts and minds. He had faith in the Lord's promise and thus the promise became more real than the reality he saw before him. Whatever the Lord has spoken to you, take faith **for it, and watch it become real.**

Mercy Seat Message #97
"Walking In Righteousness"

The Word tells us that when we accepted Jesus as Lord and Savior, God's righteousness was "imputed" to us. 'Imputed' is a term much like the bookkeeping concept of something being charged to an account like a debit or credit.

In this case, 'righteousness', which is God's absolute moral perfection, was placed into our account, wiping out the debt created by our sin nature and its sinful deeds. At that moment we became 'holy' in the sight of God, without any defilement from sin.

Our goal now is to walk out that 'absolute moral perfection' in our thoughts and actions. That which is has been placed into our account must be invested in a moral character that will cause it to increase to the glory of God. And if at any time we fall short of this, we can ask, and receive, cleansing by the blood of Jesus. And once again the slate is clean.

Mercy Seat Message #98
"Beloved I Wish Above All Things."

In 3 John the apostles' greatest prayer for the church is that we "prosper and be in health even as our <u>soul</u> prospers". Notice that our prosperity and health is connected to the prosperity of our souls.

It is important that we recognize that prosperity of the soul is the one of the highest forms of God's blessings, for from that blessing, many others flow. To have a mind renewed to the word of God, to have a will bent towards the will of God, and to have an emotional state characterized by love, peace and joy, is truly the manifestation of God's kingdom within you.

It is almost impossible to avoid the pull of material prosperity. But remember that it is still the lowest level of blessing that God bestows. If you are seeking this kingdom, as we are told by Jesus, all "these things will be added to you". In fact, if your soul is prospering the Lord will liberally add these to your life, so much so that "you will not be able to contain them". His purpose always, that you would be a blessing to many.

Mercy Seat Message #99
"Practice Makes For Perfecting"

There is a power in 'just believing' what the word of God says. Of the many precious nuggets of truth in the word of faith, is an admonition for us not to be lazy believers.

We have to take to heart the encouragement from Paul to Timothy to "study to show yourself approved...". There are some, unfortunately, who do not appropriate into their hearts and minds the life-changing 'dunamis-power' of the scriptures. And there are many who fail to apply what they have appropriated on a consistent basis. They then lack the growth in the Lord and miss the perfecting grace that it offers.

Human strength will not mold you into Christ's image and likeness. It takes action for the word to come alive in your life. Once you form the habit of practicing what is preached, you will be empowered to preach what you have practiced.

Mercy Seat Message #100
"I Have Christ In My Life"

You have probably heard someone attribute an accomplishment or achievement to "having Christ "in my life". For example, it is good to hear actors, entertainers, or athletes, honor the Lord by saying these words. You and I both know that everything good we do, or receive, is based on "having Christ in my life".

As good a profession as it is, the scriptures suggest that there is more. We are told that our lives are "hid in Christ", that we should "put on Christ", that it is "in Him we live and move and have our being". There are great blessings for those of us who "have Christ in my life". There are even greater ones available when <u>our</u> lives are <u>in</u> Christ.

The Lord doesn't just want to be in your life. He wants to be your life. He wants to live His life through you. Having Him in your life gives you answers to life's problems. Letting Him live His life through will make you a walking solution to the problems of those around you.

Mercy Seat Message #101
"No More Decisions"

Having the "mind of Christ, reminds us of our 'death' when we came into the Kingdom of God. We agreed to decrease and to allow Jesus to progressively live His life through us. We agreed to relinquish control over our purpose and direction.

Getting to that point can be easy if we remind ourselves that he wants to make all the decisions we need to have made if we would just seek Him. If we are the bride of Christ we can be assured that, as a good husband, He will make provision for all our of needs.

Today, think about those weighty decisions you are faced with. Ask yourself, which one of those you really have given up the right to make? If you seek him for direction all of the stress and anxiety over those issues will leave you. Once you decide to cast all of your cares on Him, there are no more decisions to make.

Mercy Seat Message #102
"A Heart On Fire"

You may have heard the popular Praise and Worship song called 'Shine,Jesus,Shine'. One of the lyrics is a plea for the Lord to "set our hearts on fire". When we sing it that phrase begins to burn in me. What a difference it can make in a person's outlook on life. It can become easy to do the Lord's work out of compunction or a sense of obligation. The joy quickly leaves and what used to be love turns to work.

The nearness of the Lord's blessing for your sacrifice fades and you begin to wonder, "What's the point?" If your heart is on fire, though, you never need a reason to serve. You are compelled by the awesomeness of God, and consider it a privilege to be called upon. You live and walk in a state of humility and wonder.

When you pray today join with me in asking that the hearts of all of those who call themselves "His", be set on fire. If your heart is already burning for the Kingdom of God, share it. If your flame is flickering have it ignited by this prayer for you.

Mercy Seat Message #103
"The Reward of Diligence"

Hebrews 11:6 says..."But without faith it is impossible to please him: for he that cometh to God must believe that he is, and that he is a rewarder of them that diligently seek him." Note that the 'reward' comes with the 'seeking'. To diligently seek literally means to search out with a sense of craving, like one would do if they were digging for buried treasure.

It may be helpful to remind yourself that the Lord is looking for relationship. It is possible to never miss church, to sing and pray with all your might, memorize every passage of scripture, and still miss the 'seeking' part. In all your activity this week, remember to search for Him in every thing. Remind yourself to acknowledge his presence in all of your coming and goings. He will reward you with direction, peace, wisdom, and the anointing to prosper in all you do.

Mercy Seat Message #104
"Relying On The Holy Ghost"

How much do we do <u>without</u> checking in with the Holy Ghost: 'all of the time', 'most of the time', 'some of the time', or 'hardly ever'? Thankfully none of us will raise our hands for 'hardly ever' but probably none of us can honestly say "all of the time" either.

'All the time' may not even be a realistic expectation, but it does get you thinking about increasing your access to the One whose job it is to "..teach us all things, bring all things to our remembrance... lead and guide us into all truth". So much of our worry, anxiety, and fear could be overcome if we were letting the One who knows where we ought to be going lead us.

Today, "pray" before you "do", and check in with the Holy Ghost. As Joshua learned to do before every battle (once having failed at Ai!), ask the Holy Ghost first. Before you finish your to-do list, before you make an important decision, before you plan the daily chores, before the kids get home from school, before you leave work to get on the expressway, ask the Holy Ghost what you should be doing next and know that he will help you get it done.

Mercy Seat Message #105
"Have Mercy On Me Oh God"

Psalms 51 was written following David's sin with Bathsheba. It reinforces how we should deal with any sin in our lives. Once David had been confronted by the Prophet Nathan he admitted to his shortcoming. Obviously it would have been even better to have gone to God before God came to him, but at least he did not try to deny or excuse his transgression.

In Psalms 51 he cries for God to have mercy on him and we know that a loving God heard him. Although the consequences of David's sin could not be erased, his condition of unrighteousness was. How much better we have it because of the blood of Jesus. Yes, we can cry out for God to have mercy on us when we fall short, but the truth of the Word of God is that he already has. Jesus is our mercy, sacrificed to free us from slavery to sin.

David committed physical adultery and yet our sins amount to spiritual adultery-unfaithfulness to Jesus whose bride we are. And just as Jesus said to the woman caught in the act, he says to you and I that we have been forgiven. Go and sin no more.

Mercy Seat Message #106
"Shekinah Glory"

God's expressed desire has always been to "dwell" among His people. The word used for "dwell" (shakan) conveys the idea of becoming a permanent and integral part of a community, rather than just residing somewhere. It from this concept that the Hebrew rabbis coined the word "shekinah" to describe the 'glory of God' that appeared as the shining light, the cloud, or the fire throughout the Old Testament and in the Gospels.

It is this same 'glory' that lights the holy city, New Jerusalem, in the Book of the Revelation. Except that at that point, the dwelling place (tabernacle) of God will be with men. God's expressed desire to dwell among His people and be their God will then be completely and totally fulfilled.

Mercy Seat Message #107
"Breathe On Me"

We need to more fully understand the Holy Ghost, and develop a new sense of intimacy. The receiving of the Holy Ghost at Pentecost was more than just God giving us strength or help. It was the giving of himself.

The word for "Spirit" is the Hebrew (ruach) literally meaning, "to breathe". It's what Genesis tells us the Lord did when He made Adam a living soul. It's also what Jesus did in John 20 when he breathed on the disciples and said, "receive ye the Holy Ghost."

For someone to 'breathe' on you (as supposed to touching you in any other way) is a far more intimate gesture. It also says that the Holy Ghost is the very life of God, which is imparted to us. Yes, it does give us strength and yes, it does give us help as the Comforter. But it is more than that. It is him being strong through us and him being the help that we need. The next time your choir sings "Holy Spirit, breathe on me", take in the very life of God as they sing.

Mercy Seat Message #108
"Good Acoustics"

Romans 10:17 tells us that "...faith comes by hearing, and hearing by the word of God." The word for 'hearing' is the same word from which we get our English word 'acoustics'. The sense here is that it is the quality of our hearing that produces faith, not just merely listening.

In fact the 'word of God' that we need to hear is God's voice speaking to us ('rhema') rather than the written word ('logos'). What do all of these definitions mean to you and I?

They mean that in order to be able to trust in the Lord fully we need to clearly hear Him speak to us. This type of hearing only comes from a close, personal relationship and not just a religious, routine reading of scriptures. Get in his presence today, open up your heart to hear his voice. Get close to him, that's where you'll find "good acoustics."

Mercy Seat Message #109
"Walking With A Limp"

As Jacob goes out to meet his estranged brother Esau in Genesis 32, he ends up wrestling with a "Man". Possibly an angel, this "Man" touches Jacob's thigh and causes (according to the rabbis) his sciatic nerve to shrink. From that point forward Jacob walks with a limp.

This story foretells the birth of Israel as a nation as prophesied earlier in Genesis. It also says something about us as a people of God, and how certain imperfections in our lives remind us of the need to depend even more heavily on the grace of God. Paul said in 2 Corinthians 12 that he had been given a physical infirmity to prevent him from boasting about the revelation the Lord had given him. Rather than resent his imperfection, Paul learned to glory in it, as the power of God shone through because of it.

You may be painfully aware of your own shortcomings in your walk with the Lord. And as Paul, you have probably prayed in earnest for the "limp" to be healed. Instead of despising your inability to be perfect let the power of God be made manifest in your weakness. It's okay to walk with a limp. It's just a reminder that he will steady you if you stumble and pick you up if you happen to fall.

Mercy Seat Message #110
"Questions, Questions, Questions"

Little children are famous for asking lots of questions. They want to know where they're going and continually ask 'are we there yet?' It is only as they mature that their need for answers is replaced by knowledge, based on experience.

Our walk with God is much the same it seems. When we are new in the Lord, like little children, we question much of what happens in and around us. As we grow in the things of the Lord, we will hopefully need to know less, as our experience with his faithfulness teaches us that we can trust him in all things.

Don't let the unanswered questions in your mind prevent you from taking that step the Lord has been beckoning you to take. Don't let the uncertainties you feel about your calling slow you down from moving out on his promises. Faith is the substance and evidence that you know all you need to know.. ..for now.

Mercy Seat Message #111
"The Tithe"

Naturally it takes money to live, as well as to operate a congregation. So it is easy to confuse the concept of tithing with purely financial things. And far too often the body of Christ is perceived to be overly focused on money, to the exclusion of more spiritual things.

The tithe however is all about spiritual things. The giving of the first tenth of one's increase has always been a statement of recognition that, as Psalms 24 says, "the earth is the Lord's and the fullness thereof." The tithe has always been a profession of our dependence on the Lord to take care of our needs, as the Old Testament tithe took care of the needs of the Levites, who in turn took care of the needs of the people.

Don't let any overemphasis on money within the church discourage you from honoring God with that first part of your increase. If the first part of what you have is made holy the rest will be holy.

Mercy Seat Message #112
"In His Presence"

As a believer you probably place a lot of emphasis, and value, on getting into the presence of the Lord. I certainly do. It is sweet, isn't it? That overwhelming calm. That divine sense of well-being. That 'blessed assurance' that we sometimes sing about. Funny though how our thinking often does not reflect what the Lord says about His presence.

In reality we are never <u>not</u> in God's presence. The scriptures tell us plainly that He is always there, not as a distant observer but as *Yahweh Shammah*: the ever-present one. Our mind (and those forces of darkness) want to keep us away from the reality of that "ever-present" presence. Our sins may cause us shrink from embracing that reality but the truth is that he is there.

Perhaps today you may find yourself in a place where you would think he would not be Quickly remind yourself that he never leaves us. Hopefully that will energize you in your holiness, that you would not leave Him.

Mercy Seat Message #113
"The Progressive Tabernacle"

God has worked to progressively restore fellowship with man through a series of tabernacles and temples that unfold throughout the Bible. The Tabernacle of Moses helped establish the Law, the Tabernacle of David provided a revelation of grace, and the Temple of Solomon unveiled the power of unity in worship. However, while each of these physical structures of the Old Testament provided a way for man to meet with God, they did little to dispel and atone for man's propensity to sin and sustain that fellowship in any lasting manner.

But what human effort couldn't accomplish, Jesus the Christ--the "perfect tabernacle not made with hands," and his own shed blood sprinkled on the Mercy Seat--was more than able to fulfill. Jesus was the turning point in God's plan of restoration—no longer God *among* man, but now God *in* man.

God is still building his tabernacle and he's choosing living vessels in which to dwell, and minister. There's a role that only you can play in helping to fulfill His plan for all creation. Co-labor with him in his process of building his Tabernacle in and through you.

Mercy Seat Message #114
"God's Claim"

As believers you and I know that we have been made righteous by the sacrifice of Jesus on the cross. Righteousness is the very character and nature of God himself, which, by faith, once again, he has imputed (charged to) our account.

The reality is that God has a claim on all of His creation. It all belongs to Him and it all is required to meet his demands. Those of us who are saved have simply accepted this claim and agreed to act, think, and behave accordingly. Since it is received only by grace through faith, God enables us to act, think, and behave through the indwelling power of the Holy Ghost.

What a miracle! The power of God's righteousness regenerates the human heart, soul, and mind to be able to answer the claim of an eternal Creator. 2 Corinthians 5 :17 says it best: "Therefore if any man be in Christ, he is a new creature: old things are passed away; behold, all things are become new. And all things are of God, who hath reconciled us to himself by Jesus Christ, and hath given to us the ministry of reconciliation;".

Mercy Seat Message #115
"Union Through Communion"

"...do this in remembrance of me." The word remembrance, in this case, is used not "in memory of" but in an affectionate calling of the person himself to mind. Put more plainly, be mindful of him at that moment. Since our Lord is alive and by his Spirit dwells in our hearts, we can interact directly with him. Therefore, we are able to experience him that very moment through communion.

Communing with Jesus is our life. Bringing to mind that his Life is our life and that his Life is the Light that is in us, allows him to have his way with us and others. We can walk (converse) with Him at all times. However, many of us need to be reminded. For the most part we will talk at or to God, but His desire is that we talk with Him. Therefore, we should listen and wait patiently for his sweet voice. Then by faith, we should obey what we hear.

According to Romans 10:17, faith comes by hearing and hearing by the word of God. When we hear him speak directly to us or in our situation, faith will come. Reading God's word is good, but hearing God speak his word is even more precious. Communing with God fosters union. Need quality time with Jesus? "Remember" him!

Mercy Seat Message #116
"Love The Lord..."

In Deuteronomy 6 we find the most sacred of all scriptures to the Jewish people. Deuteronomy 6:4-6 is known as the 'Shema' (the Hebrew word for 'Hear'). It should also be of equal significance to believers as it provides the most important instruction of all. We are to love the Lord our God with all of our heart, soul, and with all of our might.

This love is way beyond a warm feeling or desire for God's presence in our lives. It is the <u>action</u> of making the Lord the focus of our lives (all our heart), expressing that love with our life's vitality (soul) and keeping our relationship with him as intense as it was at the onset (all our might).

It is, above all, this relationship that the Lord desires of us. Attending church, prayer, worship, study of the Word, are all actions that <u>maintain</u> our relationship, not acquire it. Look for ways to love God today. It is an action, the response of a redeemed life.

Mercy Seat Message #117
"Reaching Perfection"

Striving for perfection in spiritual things is always a good thing. Sometimes we can complicate the matter by substituting our own standards of perfection, for those that the scriptures outline.

Jesus says in Matthew 5:43-48 that a true expression of love for God was the action of love that we show to our neighbors. He further says that to go beyond that, and show acts of love for those who are our enemies, was to be 'perfect'.

There are probably lots of situations in our lives where, even though people would not be considered 'enemies', they are clearly outside the circle of those we feel kindly towards. The unbecoming conduct of co-workers, the unsociable attitude of a neighbor, are all tremendous opportunities for us to achieve that perfection we crave. You know who they are. Now go and do something for them. You'll be perfect!.

Mercy Seat Message #118
"Self-Talk"

We know that our salvation has made us accepted by God and he now views us as righteous in his sight. Sometimes there can be a disconnect between what our hearts know and what our mind has absorbed. Often the unrenewed areas of our mind whisper negative, condemning words in our ears. This "self-talk" can become an obstacle to enjoying the depth of God's grace.

Having your mind accuse you of being a failure when you make mistakes, hearing that voice of condemnation when you struggle continually in an area of your life, being bombarded by internal criticisms of your inadequacies...these are all ways in which your self-talk can undermine the joy the Lord has imparted to you.

The only truth is what the Word of God speaks. Saturate your mind and heart with the uplifting sound of the Holy Ghost confirming through the scriptures what a marvelous work of God you are. Let his word replace that self-talk that would threaten to tear you down. Allow his truth to build you up on your most holy faith.

Mercy Seat Message #119
"Addicted To The Thrill"

In 1 Corinthians 16:15-16 Paul says, "...*I beseech you, brethren, (ye know the house of Stephanas, that it is the firstfruits of Achaia, and that they have addicted themselves to the ministry of the saints,) That ye submit yourselves unto such, and to every one that helpeth with us, and laboureth.*" He was speaking of the saints in Achaia who had given themselves over totally to the work of ministry.

This "work" is our touching (and changing) people's lives with the power of the gospel. If you have ever had the opportunity to feel that thrill it may have changed your life as well. Like the house of Stephanas we need to "addict ourselves" by engaging in the work as much as we possibly can.

There are probably those of you whose jobs or professions, though interesting, do not provide you with that thrill. Laying on your pillow after a hard day, it might be difficult to embrace the sense that what you did that day had eternal value, beyond the fact that you did it unto God. Touching and changing lives will provide that feeling. Do it frequently enough and you too will become addicted to the thrill.

Mercy Seat Message #120
"Growing Into The Priesthood"

As we mature in our relationship with the Lord, he turns our attention away from concern over our own needs to being a channel for the needs of others. In Exodus 19:4-6 God expresses his true intention for the children of Israel. If they are obedient to hear his voice and keep the covenant he has established with them, he will make them a valuable treasure and a 'kingdom of priests". Peter, as I mentioned earlier, reiterates our priesthood calling in the New Testament.

The priesthood was established to minister to the Lord and to enter his presence to make atonement for the needs of the people. We too, who have a revelation of our role, are given the honor of taking the needs of unsaved people before the throne, as well as the needs of saved people who do not yet possess such a revelation.

The priesthood was "set apart" from the rest of the people to devote themselves to this service. We too must allow the process of sanctification to set us apart, as we grow away from attention to "self" to attending to others. As with the Old Testament priesthood, our portion is the presence of the Lord. As we enter in, he meets our needs with overflowing abundance honoring our sacrifice to be obedient to hear his voice and be that channel of blessing for others.

Mercy Seat Message #121
"You Are Where You Live"

Whether you are good friends, husband and wife, or parent and child, each of these relationships has 'terms'. As with husband and wife, if they agree to the terms of their marriage, their relationship will be wholesome and fulfilling.

Paul tells us in several places in Romans that if we live in constant contact with the Holy Ghost, then we will be "spiritual people". Conversely, if we live in obedience to the demands and desires of our human nature, we will be "carnal people". It really is that simple. To be spiritually-minded, he says, brings us life and peace. But to be focused on carnal things brings decay and emptiness.

In other words, you are where you live. If you spend your time thinking about all the negative things in your life, and in the lives of others, negativity will abound. Meditate on God's power to sustain the good, and change the not-so-good, then just watch the goodness become you .

Mercy Seat Message #122
"Wisdom And Revelation"

For an entire month the Lord prompted our congregation to begin our Sunday worship by reading together Ephesians 1:17-23. These verses are a prayer by Paul that the Lord would "give you a spirit of wisdom and revelation in the knowledge of Him." We have found that this prayer has evoked a deeper commitment to acquiring the revelation that Paul was praying for. Sometimes it seems that we can be satisfied with what we know about him and lose the "energy" to deepen our intimacy.

Some folks may even be surprised that there is wisdom and revelation of him available. If God is just a passive force in the universe and not "someone" who you can get to know, then what is the need for more revelation? Or if we think we know all about him that there is to know, why pursue it even further? You'd have to admit that it's a good thing to know him at all, and we would be foolish to criticize anyone who doesn't agree that there is more. At the same time, if Paul is praying for something, you'd have to believe we might want to receive it.

This 'revelation' may be the increased awareness of how much he cares about you. It may the powerful reminder that your lack of perfection will not cause Him to love you less. Or the revelation may be of the profound purpose for which he saved you. Regardless of what it is, Paul wants you to have it. And so do I. Go for it.

Mercy Seat Message #123
"Plan and Purpose-Food For Thought"

Most believers are aware of the importance of renewing our minds. Romans 12:1-5 tells us about the transformation process that needs to take place in order to prove out the "good, acceptable, and perfect will of God". What is interesting is that if you read Romans 11 carefully you may get some new insight into the "therefore" in Romans 12:1.

Essentially Paul reminds us that God's chosen people, the Jewish people, were "replaced" by us Gentiles. The covenant promise of being His people was taken from them and given to us. Lest we get carried away with ourselves Paul further reminds us that if God removed those originally chosen from their place of blessing, why would he hesitate to remove the "second choice"? He also assures us that the gifts and callings are without repentance and he will certainly honor His promise to the Jewish people. (You have to really love them. Their steadfastness in keeping the word alive is a great treasure.)

In fact, it is through our obedience to the Lord's will that the Jewish people are returned to their rightful place. Hence the renewing of our minds, and subsequent transformation, is not just so we can prosper and acquire more material possessions. It is so that God's plan for the redemption of all mankind can take place. That should give you and I some food for thought about His plan and our purpose.

Mercy Seat Message #124
"Whose Will?"

The night that he was betrayed Jesus took His disciples to their frequent place of prayer, the garden of Gethsemane on the Mount of Olives. It was there that he fervently called out to God as he prepared himself for the events that were to take place. Recall that Jesus asked, in simple terms, that if there was a way to change His fate, He would opt for it, but otherwise, he would embrace God's will.

Gethsemane was actually a place where the olives from the orchard were pressed to make the precious oil so vital to all aspects of life in that part of the world. The oil was used for light, for the anointing oil in the temple, as well as for making soap, cosmetics, and cooking. It was at the olive press that Jesus made the decision that God's will was more important to him than his own. You and I will often find ourselves at our own "Gethsemane". As the Spirit of God continues to sanctify us to his purposes, we face the choice of hanging on to what we want, or letting go and accepting that which the Lord has ordained for us.

The 'olive press' is an uncomfortable place for sure. But you can read in John 18, for example, that after Jesus has accepted his place, the 'anointing oil' flows with such power that even the Roman soldiers fall on their face before him at the mention of who he is. Choose his will. No matter how difficult the path he is asking you to travel may seem, choose it. His anointing will flow and your enemies, your problems, and your circumstances will fall at your feet.

Trumpet Blast #125
"Who Gets The Worship?"

The word for "worship" refers to the act of bowing before one who is superior in authority or power, and worthy of honoring. Often we are unaware of the seriousness of our casual acts of forgetfulness about the things of God.

Our culture seems to suggest that you have a choice of either worshipping the Lord, worshipping the devil or not worshipping at all! The scriptures appear to teach us something different. Both Old and New Testament make it rather clear that there is no "in-between", that you are always "worshipping one or the other."

That concept may change some of your behaviors and make you more conscious of walking in holiness before the Lord. A tendency to be casual about keeping the instructions of the Lord may in fact be an act of worship of the evil one, as we bow down to serve our selfless lusts and desires. As Jesus clearly told Satan in the wilderness, we worship only the Lord. He is the one we bow down to.

Mercy Seat Message #126
"On This Rock"

Remember once again in Matthew 16 when the disciples are asked by Jesus who people said that He was. Among the responses is Peter's who, with some apparent astonishment, says that he is the Christ, the Son of the Living God. Jesus says that upon this rock the church will be built. What 'rock' would that be?

Here's my two cents. No one told Peter who Jesus really was, as much as it was revealed to him. After months of following Jesus and seeing him work miracles, Peter's eyes were opened to see that he was the Messiah, God's promised Savior. He had always been God's promised Savior, but it took a moment of revelation for Peter to really "see".

Sometimes we could use a moment of revelation to really "see". There are miracles of God happening all around us. In your workplace, in your family, even in your life, God continues to work and to will of his good pleasure. We can get so caught up in the issues that we fail to see those miracles. We can fail to see the Christ, the Son of the Living God, right in front of us. Don't let this day pass without some revelation. It is the rock upon which God is also building you up as a member of his church. And the gates of hell will not stand against you either.

Mercy Seat Message #127
"No Condemnation"

Romans 8:1 makes it clear that guilt and shame have no place in the life of a believer. That's hard for the "religious" mind to comprehend. The notion of the price being already paid goes against the grain of our human nature. That nature would rather exact some sort of punishment for wrongdoing.

God's way of dealing with our sin is to love us to the point where we chose to allow Him to be the satisfier of the need that our sin is trying to satisfy. Hear that again. *God's way of dealing with our sin is to love us to the point where we choose to allow Him to be the satisfier of the need that our sin is trying to satisfy.*

At some point today you may fall short of the will of God. Your 'feeling bad' should be a trigger, not to feel guilt and shame, but to feel God's love and forgiveness. That love should lead you to repentance (a change of mind) that will enhance your ability to obey.

Mercy Seat Message #128
"Not By Bread Alone"

As we grow in the Lord and our intimacy with God increases, we learn to seek him regularly in prayer and intercession. As we mature more spiritually, praying becomes as much a time for listening as it is for speaking. We begin to know that we need to hear what God is saying to us as we communicate our needs to him.

During the temptation in the wilderness as recorded in the gospels, Jesus told Satan, "*It is written, Man shall not live by bread alone, but by every word that proceedeth out of the mouth of God.*" The literal meaning of 'word' is a living voice rather than something that is put in writing. That is not to say that the written word does not reflect the voice of a living God. It simply suggests that there is a written word (logos) and a spoken (rhema) by which God communicates to us through. Both are the source of our life.

When you seek him today be sure to listen. The spirit of God desires to provide us with the instructions, insight, and wisdom to "live" our lives to the fullness of his divine purpose. He desires to equip us with the knowledge, direction, and perspective to see and act upon things from his point of view.

Mercy Seat Message #129
"I Do"

Standing at the edge of Mount Sinai the Jewish people responded favorably to the Lord's proposal to take them unto himself. In Exodus 19:5-6 the terms of the betrothal are expressed as "...Now therefore, if ye will obey my voice indeed, and keep my covenant, then ye shall be a peculiar treasure unto me above all people: for all the earth is mine: And ye shall be unto me a kingdom of priests, and an holy nation".

Their excitement doesn't last long unfortunately. As the Lord returns in the noise and thick smoke, they now back away, asking Moses to hear what the Lord has to say as they are afraid to approach Him. They also back away from their vow to listen to his voice and cripple their ability to keep His covenant.

You and I have also said "I do". When we asked Jesus to be our Lord and Savior we acknowledged that a price was paid for our becoming his bride. You and I agreed to the terms of the union. We agreed to obey his voice and keep his covenant. And like our Jewish ancestors we can face that same challenge of wanting to back away from time to time, when he wants to speak to us.

If we are to truly be the Bride of Christ we must trust the Groom. We must know in our hearts that he has also made a promise in saying "I do". He has promised to never leave or forsake you. He has promised to lead you in paths of righteousness for the sake of His own name. And he, more than any other, will always keep his word. It has been sealed in his own blood.

Mercy Seat Message #130
"Following The Law"

This issue of the "keeping the Law" has been confusing Christians for centuries, largely because we don't really comprehend what he is talking about or why. For example, if "law" was translated as "instructions" and if "keep" was rendered as "to guard and protect", would there really be a problem?

There really should be little reason to debate it. In fact, Jesus himself said in John 14:15," *If ye love me, keep my commandments.*" We certainly don't keep God's laws <u>to be</u> saved but we do keep them <u>because</u> we are saved. The Holy Ghost has been given to us to lead and guide us towards the establishing and maintenance of Godly behavior in our thoughts, attitudes, and actions.

Many people have noted that the Ten Commandments, as a summary of the law, seem nothing more than a list of do's and don'ts. It is clearly much more than that. That word used for "instructions" is the word 'torah' which literally means "to hit the mark", like an arrow reaching the target. Torah conveys the idea of "that which is really going on". In other words, God's "do's and don'ts" direct us to Godly behavior in our thoughts, attitudes, and actions, that produce blessings in ways we cannot often comprehend.

The guarding and protecting of God's instructions is not a slavish obedience to rituals and regulations that cannot produce life, but it is a submitted obedience to the Author and Creator of life. There is just no way around our need and obligation to be obedient. Do so, and it will produce blessing. Ignore it, and your way will be made hard....or worse.

Mercy Seat Message #131
"No Graven Images"

The second commandment is spelled out beginning in Exodus 20:4," Thou shalt not make unto thee any graven image, or any likeness of any thing that is in heaven above, or that is in the earth beneath, or that is in the water under the earth:". While the reference to idols is clear there is much more under the surface.

While the first commandment ("No other gods...) focuses on <u>who</u> is to be worshipped, the second relates to <u>how</u> to worship.

Likenesses of God pertain not only to statues or icons but to anything that interferes with the way God wants to be worshipped. As the God who showed grace on Israel by delivering them from the bondage of Egypt, the Lord desires a personal form of worship. Let not anything come between you and an intimate, "face-to-face", conversation and communion with the Holy One. Tear down any religious thought that suggests that the blood of Jesus was not enough to cause you to be worthy of acceptance by God.

Dismantle every demonic altar that gets in the way of your understanding his desire to have you in his presence. He is, as he says, a jealous God and craves the undivided attention of his Bride. Abandon any silly notion that while God may <u>love you</u>, he may not necessarily <u>like you.</u> Bow down and worship only him. Give him the glory that is due his name. That glory is what you possess, provided to you by Jesus' sacrifice on the cross. Give him the glory by giving yourself in worship.

Mercy Seat Message #132
"Unto Us"

In the ninth chapter the prophet Isaiah speaks of the coming Messiah-:6 "For unto us a child is born, unto us a son is given: and the government shall be upon his shoulder: and his name shall be called Wonderful, Counsellor, The mighty God, The everlasting Father, The Prince of Peace. "Jesus is no longer a babe in a manger but the glorified Son of God, reigning in preeminence over all creation and awaiting the command for his return. But yet, every day, every hour, unto us a child is born and unto us a Son is given. You see, the Spirit of God is being continually birthed in us with the freshness and newness of that crispy night in the town of Bethlehem. God's mercies are new to us every morning.

The real power of believing in Jesus is the operation of God's grace in our lives. Because of the years of religious indoctrination that most of us have been exposed to, it is hard sometimes to really comprehend grace. We don't mean just understanding the concept but having it "birthed" in our hearts. Birthed to such an extent that we can live our lives in relation to the knowledge of grace working in and around us.

The baby in the barn came to reveal that God's love would be the operative method of dealing with man's sinfulness. His birth was a proclamation that the wages of sin would still be death but that he had come to die in our place. He had come to show us that God planned to love us out of sinfulness into holiness. Unto us, the Messiah gave us life by taking the penalty for our criminal trespass. Unto him, we need to live our lives in grateful thanksgiving for His love.....not just in celebration of his birth but in humble acknowledge of his endless life.

Mercy Seat Message #133
"Narrow-Minded Christians"

You may have already heard sources, like the media, refer to committed Christians as being "narrow-minded". In our culture today that is a serious indictment that one might not be accepting of any idea that's different from their own.

While the love that we have for all people enables us to show tolerance for others and their beliefs, being "narrow-minded" is actually a tremendous compliment if you consider the words of Jesus. He said..."wide is gate and broad is the way that leads to destruction and many there be that go in thereat. But strait is the gate and narrow is the way that leads to life, and few there be that even find it."

As Christians we have intentionally chosen the "narrow way". There are thoughts, behaviors, ideas concepts, and values that are destructive to spiritual life. We have to make intelligent decisions about what to allow into our frame of reference. We have to screen out that which is evil and cling to that which is good. We are called to cast down vain imaginations and anything that exalts itself against the knowledge of God.

To think that all ideas and approaches are equally beneficial is foolish. Be tolerant? Yes, absolutely. Accept everything as valuable and healthy? Not hardly. The next time you hear us referred to as narrow-minded think of the words of Jesus and rejoice.

Mercy Seat Message #134
"Taking The Tour"

Imagine being led on a tour of a museum, historical site, or other venue by a guide with years and years of experience in walking people through the wonders of the location. Imagine at every stop you interrupt the guide and question: "...where are we going next???", "are you really sure you know how to get us there???", "do you really know what you're talking about?", "how much longer until we're at the end of the tour?", and on and on.

If you're starting to think that you and I are sometimes that nervous person on the tour, continually questioning the Holy Ghost (our tour guide in this life) you're getting the point. Jeremiah 29:11 says, "For I know the thoughts that I think toward you, saith the Lord, thoughts of peace and not of evil, to give you an expected end."

Just as the pillar of smoke and the column of fire led the children of Israel, the Holy Ghost knows the way out of our personal wilderness. Instead of questioning so much, we need to trust the tour guide more. He's been leading people on this since eternity, and no one has ever been disappointed or asked for their money back.

Mercy Seat Message #135
"Whose Life Is It Anyway?"

When you accepted Jesus as your Savior you made a 'trade'. You allowed him to pay the penalty incurred by the debt of your sin nature in exchange for his right to live his life through you. It is really important for you to incorporate this reality into your everyday thought process.

The new creation that you have become exists as a vessel to contain the life of God, in the name of Jesus, operated by the power of the Holy Ghost. All decisions that are made for your life must be filtered through the will of God or else you run the risk of misusing the vessel and dishonoring the agreement. God's promise is to bless the vessel, and its use in this life, as well as in the life to come. If you follow this pattern you will never have to worry about striving for mastery over your life or the circumstances you confront. He will take care of them all.

It is noteworthy again that several times in the Gospels Jesus says "...*For whosoever will save his life shall lose it: but whosoever will lose his life for my sake, the same shall save it.* " If we fail to remember that is actually his life we will be motivated to do the things that hold onto that which is in us, rather than allowing it to be poured out on behalf of others. Remember, only when we allow the bread to be broken can the multitudes be fed. And only when they are fed, will we truly eat.

Mercy Seat Message #136
"Blind Minds"

1 Corinthians 4 tells us that the "god this world has blinded the minds of unbelievers....". This apparently refers to the manner in which the forces of darkness that penetrate the earth, have cast a pall of ignorance over the world. The truth is that everyone has been saved. It's just that so many are "blind" to the truth of God's omnipotence, the severity of his law, and the propitiation that Jesus made for their law-breaking.

Satan and the host of demonic powers that are allied together have woven a web of illusion about the things of this world. Despite the fact that everyone knows we are only here temporarily, they are seduced into clutching onto this life as if it were permanent. They are seduced into working hard to acquire as many 'things' as they can, full-well knowing that they bring only short term gratification.

It is into this blindness that you and are cast, with the illuminating light of God's Word and the presence of His Holy Ghost within us. We cannot afford to lose sight of the fact that those around us who do not know him are not "bad" people, just "blind" people. We should treat them as we would any sightless individual. Remove any dangerous obstacles set before them when they walk. Guide them gently when they ask for a hand. And warn them of the danger that lies ahead.

Mercy Seat Message #137
"Demonization"

In this age of horror movies and spectacular special effects, the notion of demonic forces has become almost comical. Yet from a Biblical perspective, it is an inescapable reality. While concern over the devil and the work of demons can be greatly overdone it is equally irresponsible to pretend as if it is not a real thing.

Much of the sickness, disease, conflict and violence in our society comes from the influence of this veil of evil, which apparently exists in the same realm as the "good guys", our guardian angels. These evil forces have the ability to direct the behavior of anyone whose lifestyle is full of sin and lawlessness. While theologians debate whether demons can possess believers, the sad truth is that if you are not walking in holiness, their influence can "demonize" your behavior to the point that it really doesn't matter what we call it.

Holiness, therefore, is the key. Armed with the righteousness of God through Christ Jesus, we need not fear demons, in fact, they need to fear us. Remember what it says in 2 Corinthians 10:3-5:, "For though we walk in the flesh, we do not war after the flesh: (For the weapons of our warfare are not carnal, but mighty through God to the pulling down of strong holds; Casting down imaginations, and every high thing that exalteth itself against the knowledge of God, and bringing into captivity every thought to the obedience of Christ."

Mercy Seat Message #138
"More Than Conquerors Are We"

We know from the word that we are called by God as Christians to be conquerors. But what do we conquer and how?

Well, for one, we can be conquerors over the "pressure of our past" and its ability to rob us of our present and destroy the hope of our future. People without Christ (and sadly, many who know the Lord) live every day with the cloud of their past experiences limiting their lives. As Christians we know that "old things have passed away and all things are become new."

Second, we can conquer our inability to "control the outcomes" of our life experiences. Most people dare not admit that they cannot control events yet live with the sadness of knowing deep in their hearts that they actually are altogether helpless. We know that in Christ we can lean on the Lord. We know that God already has a plan for our lives that we can trust in.

Finally, we conquer the "emptiness of our imperfection". Deep down we all know that based on our sin nature we are pretty "rotten" people. That is, our own goodness was temporary at best and quite inconsistent. In Christ we know that God will love through us, forgive through us, and show mercy to us. We are released from trying to be good people and let the perfection of Christ in us affect those around us.

Today, remember Romans 8:37-..."nay in all things we are more than conquerors through him that loved us."

Part III

TIMES AND SEASONS

I have learned so much from other ministers, especially my wife and co-pastor, Rev. Rita Thompson and the Global Truth Ministries' elders, Pearlie Madkins and Carol Madkins. I know the quality and integrity of their walk with the Lord. In my subconscious mind that has qualified them to not only to speak into my life directly but for me to see the importance of gleaning from them even as they minister to others. They continue to leave the footprints of their walk in the sand of my life that I might follow, imitating them as they imitate the Christ.

Our church has always recognized the value of the Feasts of Israel and these have served as spiritual markers in the seasons of my relationship with the Lord. These feasts are never celebrated as religious observances, but as sources of revelation and powerful object lessons about salvation. I have found them perhaps even more inspiring than our traditional religious and cultural observations throughout the year. You may discover that the Lord has deposited a lot of revelation in his celebrations, which can be applied to the phases and cycles of your natural and spiritual life.

Mercy Seat Message #139
"Thanks-Giving"

Thanks-giving. When we get to late November everyone's attention is focused on the theme of thanksgiving and rightly so. It is also a good time to bring ourselves into the remembrance of what thanks-giving means to us as believers. The Bible tells us that it is a good thing to give thanks unto the Lord. Of course the scriptures are not talking about our annual holiday but a mindset and a lifestyle that expresses thankfulness to God for all aspects of his work in our lives.

While most of us will give thanks through prayer or attending a church service, God's real expectation is that we thank him in many other ways as well. We can thank God by living in holiness, "eschewing (avoiding) evil" and doing good. We can thank him by sharing the good news of the gospel with those whose souls dwell in darkness. We can show our thanks to God by operating fully in the gifting he has given to us.

The point is that our lives should be a continual expression of thanks for the goodness of God. He is blessing us at all times whether we can see it or not. Yes, give thanks on that special Thursday. Make it a special time for you, your family and friends. (Eat plenty of turkey and stuffing, too but don't hurt yourself!) And make it a point also to commit your life as an expression of thanks-giving everyday, from now until he comes.

Mercy Seat Message #140
"Feast of Tabernacles"

The feasts of the Lord are a special time in the Body of Christ. In Passover we can see Jesus as the Lamb of God who was slain. At Pentecost we can see the giving of the Holy Ghost. In the season of Tabernacles we can see the ingathering of God's people and the soon-coming King.

Tabernacles is actually three feasts: Trumpets, Atonement, and Tabernacles itself. On the day of Trumpets we can hear the shofar announce that the Day of Atonement (Yom Kippur to the

Jewish people) is approaching. On that great day, at the sound of the last trump, it will be announced that he who WAS the atonement, is returning for his Bride, the Church. On Tabernacles the children of Israel built booths and celebrated for seven days. When he returns we too will dwell with him in perfection for eternity.

For us as believers, keeping the feasts of the Lord is a spiritual celebration, not the ritualistic ceremony of the Old Testament. The season of the feasts is also a time when the Spirit of God brings forth a harvest to his people who have opened their hearts to see Jesus.

Mercy Seat Message #141
"Looking for Jesus"

Our congregation was treated to a musical play in which characters took turns knocking on a Christians' door, asking for water, for directions, for help with their various needs and so on. Each time the devout woman refused to help because she was "looking for Jesus" to visit her home and had to get ready for his soon coming.

At the conclusion Jesus did finally come to her house, only to let her know that he had been there numerous times that day. As an ex-con for whom she had no compassion, as a homeless person for whom she would give no shelter, as a thirsty person for whom she would give no water..... In Matthew 25 such believers are cast into everlasting punishment.

Lest we leave this thought as a parable or as the plot of a nice play, think of how often in the hustle and bustle of our daily lives we fail to take the time to see Jesus as the co-worker distraught with family problems, the neighbor who drinks too much, or the cousin in another state that no one in the family wastes their time with anymore. The scripture explains that as we have done kindnesses to the least of our brethren we have done them to Jesus.

Sure there are dangers in helping strangers and the Lord would expect you to use wisdom in opening your hand or house. But keep looking for Jesus as the time of his coming draws near. And don't forget to recognize him when he comes your way.

Mercy Seat Message #142
"A Daily Pentecost"

Pentecost, the second of the three Feasts of the Lord, occurs 50 days after Passover. There are some powerful symbols in the Old Testament, which speak of its fulfillment in the New Testament.

In Exodus 19 (right before the 10 commandments are given) the children of Israel balk at coming near the presence of God. He wants them to become a "kingdom of priests" and, while initially enthusiastic, they ultimately cannot handle the idea for fear of the fire and thunder that the Lord appears in. A good lesson for us-do not fear to draw near to his glory.

In the New Testament, God's quest for intimacy is fulfilled. In Acts 2 the Holy Ghost, promised by Jesus, descends and infills the believers who are gathered. More than a source of spiritual gifts, the Holy Ghost is the vehicle by which we get to know God better. We can finally know him because now he lives in us.

The lesson for us is that Pentecost is not an event but a process. Rather than a once-a-year encounter, everyday should be a Pentecost, as we seek to get to know him better on a continuous basis. After all, one day when Christ returns, we will be like him.

Mercy Seat Message #143
"The Gift of Family"

Just recently I had found myself at the airport's international arrival gate. I was among at least four to five hundred people waiting anxiously for their loved ones, most of whom were family members who had been separated for some time.

It was not uncommon for those who were waiting to make a mad dash down the wide corridor as soon as they saw their family member emerge through the doors leading into the waiting area. Numerous times I saw both take off running toward each other as that hug and kiss could not be delayed one more second. Once a young woman who was reuniting with her parents (I assume) let her luggage cart go as she ran to embrace them. The cart crashed into the walls and her belongings were strewn all over. But it was her family that mattered at that moment, not her stuff.

I could not help think, as many of us held back tears just watching these scenes, about the body of Christ. We have the opportunity to create this same sense of family. Perhaps we will not come running down the aisles when we see one another come through the church doors but we can let each other know that we are just as glad to be together. And maybe one day, like the young woman, we may even be willing to abandon all of our stuff for each other's love.

Mercy Seat Message #144
"Call On Him"

One of our ministers shared an inspiring word with us on the indwelling presence of God. He pointed out that the Holy Ghost was sent to us, in the words of Jesus, as "another Helper". Just as we all called on the Lord to be saved, Pastor Nolan encouraged us to call on the Holy Spirit for help in all of the tasks and circumstances that we face. It is the desire, if you will, of the Holy Spirit to be called upon, to be used.

If you are facing a pressure-filled meeting today, ask the Holy Spirit to accompany you and give you the words to speak. The meeting is perhaps trivial in the grand scheme of things but the fact you must face it makes it important to the Lord.

If you have to decipher the complexities of a stack of budget figures today, ask the Holy Spirit to give you the wisdom and the understanding. No, the budget is not critical to the kingdom of God, but the fact that you must decipher it makes it important to the Lord.

If there is dirty laundry, dirty dishes, dirty floors, and dirty faces that you must clean today, ask the Holy Spirit to give you patience, energy, and anointing to see His purposes in it. No, dirty dishes are not a key factor in the Lord's plan, but if you have to clean them, He cares.

Call on Him today. Right now. He is waiting to be used.

Mercy Seat Message #145
"Justice For All?"

Our social and political environment champions the value of justice---making sure that the guilty pay for their crimes. Pastor Rita Thompson shared with us a stirring message on the important distinction between justice and justification.

You see, it turns out we had all committed the worst crime possible, having once been alienated from God. We were charged with the full penalty of our sin. Many of us sat on death row until we accepted the Son of God's offer to take our punishment for us. Now having received a pardon from the Lord we can live our lives, not as ex-cons, but as his righteousness. We have been justified because Jesus endured God's justice on our behalf.

If you have trouble finding something today to be thankful for (days can be like that sometimes can't they?) thank the Lord for sparing you the penalty of your sin.

Mercy Seat Message #146
"Whose Opinion?"

Remember the Florida election coverage awhile back? I recall hearing the numerous opinions of who should do what and why. It seems so much of our culture revolves around whose opinion we should listen to.

Opinions can be dangerous things. Such as an opinion on what kind of person you are or whether God will bless you or what it takes for the Lord to respond to your needs. The answers to these are all subjective-meaning your disposition or present circumstances could affect your point of view.

God's "opinion" is the only one that is not subjective. His word is sure and his view of you and I is fixed in relation to the blood of Jesus. He says you are his righteousness because of Jesus. He says that before the foundation of the world he laid out a plan for your life. He says that you can do all things through Christ which strengthens you.

So whenever you need an opinion, cast your vote for the word of God and the many blessings he has promised you. There will never be a recount.

Mercy Seat Message #147
"Dead to Sin"

In a Sunday service Pastor Rita Thompson reminded us of our being "dead" to sin according to Romans 6. On one hand being "dead" removes all of our excuses for our failure to live in holiness. We can't say, for example, that the 'devil made me do it', because the devil cannot make a dead person do anything. Rather, we are left to confront our will and fleshly appetites. There is however, good news.

Just as it was the power of God that raised us up with him in the likeness of his resurrection, it is the same power that causes us to participate in his crucifixion. In other words God himself will deliver you from your inability to live in holiness. It will never be by your own strength.

When John the Baptist said, "the axe has been laid to the root of the tree" he was perhaps making a profound comment on sinfulness, saying that the Lord would remove the root cause of it from us. Today, let the Spirit of the living God remove the need that is producing whatever sin is besetting you. Live in him and therefore be dead to sin.

Mercy Seat Message #148
"Unto Us A Child Is Born"

A couple of years ago our annual Christmas Celebration focused on the words of Isaiah-"... unto us a child is born". Jesus is no longer a babe in a manger but the glorified Son of God, reigning in preeminence over all creation and awaiting the command for His return. But yet in still, every day, every hour, unto us a child is born and unto us a Son is given. You see, the Spirit of God is being continually birthed in us with the freshness and newness of that crispy night in the town of Bethlehem. God's mercies are new to us every morning.

The real power of believing in Jesus is the operation of God's grace in our lives. Because of the years of religious indoctrination that most of us have been exposed to, it is hard sometimes to really comprehend grace. We don't mean just understanding the concept but having it "birthed" in our hearts. Birthed to such an extent that we can live our lives in relation to the knowledge of grace working in and around us.

The baby in the barn came to reveal that God's love would be the operative method of dealing with man's sinfulness. His birth was a proclamation that the wages of sin would still be death but He had come to die in our place. He had come to show us that God planned to love us out of sinfulness into holiness.

Mercy Seat Message #149
"A New Years' Revolution"

Every January 2nd or 3rd lots of people return to work, or begin their list of chores, with a well-intentioned plan to fix something in their lives that hasn't been working. While that's a noble effort it will probably takes lots of will power and, if successful, they will undoubtedly struggle to maintain it.

As believers we have something even more potent and permanent. Rather than fixing things with 'will' power, we can be transformed through Holy Ghost power. It is effortless, and will last an eternity. It is maintained by God's ability to sustain it, as one who Peter claims is "able to keep us from falling".

The work of the Lord in our lives is designed to bring us into the fullness of the nature of the stature of Christ. This is not just a linear, incremental, fix-up. It is the continual bringing forth of something brand new. It is a revolution.

Mercy Seat Message #150
"Nothing Can Separate Us"

What a blessing our congregation encountered when Rev. Gerald Mayhan and his wife, Phyllis, shared a message and testimony on Romans 8:31 and following. Their life example was an incredible encouragement in the power of prayer and the unfailing commitment the Lord has in bringing us to the place he wants us to be.

To make a long story short, Gerald and Phyllis endured 18 years (!) of his drug addiction before, as he says, he "figured it out" and gave his life to Christ. She not only stood in prayer but gave him up to the power of God, believing God would bring her husband back to her as a man of God.

It should encourage anyone's heart to know that the word "impossible" is not in the Lord's vocabulary and that no matter how desperate it seems to us, his plan cannot be thwarted. "Nothing can separate you from the love of God". If it seems far-fetched just ask Gerald and Phyllis.

Mercy Seat Message #151
"The Blessing of Service"

Certainly there could be any number reasons why, at some points in time, things 'dry up' in our spiritual lives. One of the more common causes for this dryness though can be our lack of service towards others.

In one of our Sunday Services Pastor Rita Thompson reminded of us of how serving activates the "body ministry" in the Kingdom of God. That means that when we serve others the Lord 'releases' the blessings that are stored up for us.

You may be in that dry place right now or possibly know someone else who is. Be encouraged that the solution to your own problems can always be your being the solution to someone else's. If you need the Lord to rain down his glory on you, then shed the light of his love on another.

Mercy Seat Message #152
"If The Foundations Be Destroyed…"

The public debate over abortion, sexual preferences, or genetics seems to have much of the body of Christ distracted. Many are concerned, and rightly so, about taking sides on these questions but mainly from a political perspective. These issues are anything but political. They are all about the power of sin.

You see sin is, as always, trying to get us to agree that it is the will of 'man' and not the will of God that governs right versus wrong. If a person can decide that life begins in the womb rather than in the mind of God (before the foundation of the world), we can then choose whether it lives or dies by our hand. If we agree that your sexual preference is determined by passions that you cannot control because they are in your DNA, then it is not the power of God that upholds one's choices and governs those same passions.

Clearly it is important for believers to take a stand. But it is not 'flesh and blood' that we are wrestling against, but principalities and powers. Our freedom as a nation depends on our being clear about the real problem and the real enemy. We need more love for the human perpetrators of these lies and more hatred for the source of them….sin.

Mercy Seat Message #153
"Knowing Versus Believing"

Elder Pearlie Madkins gave us some inspired teaching one Sunday, concerning the depth of the Lord's love for us. She caused us to ponder the difference between 'knowing' he loves you, versus 'believing' he loves you. 'Knowing' helps you to endure while 'believing' will enable you to overcome.

'Belief' comes from a level of intimate contact with Jesus, doing what the book of Hebrews suggests as "considering" the High Priest of our confession. By "considering" it means that we ponder the depths of who Jesus is the way an astronomer studies the stars. We take time out from our busy day to simply think on him and the wonders of his love. We recall to our minds the many ways he has delivered us from evil and led us away from temptation.

'Knowing' he loves you is a good first step. Take that knowledge and 'consider' him. He will birth in your heart a new level of understanding, the life-changing intimacy of 'believing'.

Mercy Seat Message #154
"We Fall Down"…(and He Picks Up)"

"We fall down but we get up. For a saint is just a sinner who fell down, and got up."

You may have heard this song- a very moving popular contemporary Christian lyric. If you understand the mercy of God you would know that even this beautiful song cannot capture the real story.

Yes, we fall down but it is really the Lord who gets us up. His love for us extends beyond our shortcomings and it is always his desire that we walk in blessing. When we fall down he stretches forth his hand to raise us up.

And in fact, if you are a saint, you are much more than just a sinner who got up. You are someone who made a quality decision to allow the resurrecting power of Jesus to govern your life. You are a special person who has chosen to let him be your life.

We fall down, but as Jude says "Now unto him that is able to keep you from falling, and to present you faultless before the presence of his glory with exceeding joy, To the only wise God our Savior, be glory and majesty, dominion and power, both now and for ever. Amen."

Mercy Seat Message #155
"My House Is Full"

At the Basin Street Gospel Brunch in Sterling, Virginia, our Rev. Betty Fluker sang a song about the Lord's house (the church on Sunday morning) being full but the Lord's harvest fields being empty of laborers.

It was an encouragement that, as the Body of Christ, we try not to consider attending church as our witness to the Lord, but rather our laboring in the vineyards among those who do not know him.

Church services are wonderful and we should have a full house every time the doors open. But that person in the other cubicle or the one across the street may never enter a church. And if they do there is a chance they will still not hear the words of redemption through the blood of Jesus.

As you may have heard many times, your life may be the only Bible that someone ever sees. Open it and share the Word.

Mercy Seat Message #156
"Dedicated to the Lord"

Baby dedications are special moments at church. In most dedications the parents want to make public their acknowledgment that their little one is a gift from God and that they are grateful stewards of that gift. We then pray that the Lord will keep his hand upon them and that he would establish his covenant with them as the child grows to the age of decision-making.

As we speak these words I'm always reminded of our regular need to 'dedicate' ourselves to the Lord. We need to regularly acknowledge that our lives and possessions are gifts from him, and that we are to be faithful stewards over these gifts. We need him to establish the freshness of our covenant with Him and remind us of the unbreakable promises in his Word, ratified by the blood of Jesus.

God's desire for you is that you bear fruit for his kingdom. As you dedicate yourself and all that you have to his service, you will truly be the branch as he is the Vine.

Mercy Seat Message #157
"How to Abide"

At a Pentagon Women's Bible Study Retreat, Pastor Derrell Emerson of Christian Assembly in Vienna, Virginia, shared an outstanding message on the importance of 'abiding' with Jesus. This 'abiding' is not just the fellowship with Him in a church service or in reading the Bible (all good things to do) but in enjoying a vital interaction with the Lord.

Pastor Derrell encouraged us to treat every moment as a place where we can meet God. "Right now" is the only time we are given. It is foolish to wait for another moment to touch the Lord. As you sit there at your desk or make copies at the xerox machine or drive across town on an errand, the moment is "now" to feel the Lord's presence.

Don't 'under-spiritualize' the common tasks of your daily life as if the Lord is not available in the midst of your doing. Washing dishes, cutting the grass, or cooking dinner are all prime places for the Lord's presence to be felt. In fact, think about this.... they are the only places on this side of glory, where you and he can meet!!! As Jesus said, "If ye abide in me, and my words abide in you, ye shall ask what ye will, and it shall be done unto you".

Mercy Seat Message #158
"Independence Day"

Each 4th of July we celebrate our country's anniversary of independence from the tyranny of men. It is a great time to reflect on the blessings of living in a society whose principles are based on the self-governing ability of people under the rule of law. Interestingly enough, these ideas apply to us as believers.

We could logically celebrate the event of our personal salvation as a type of "Dependence Day". For when you asked Jesus to be your Lord and Savior you too were freed of tyranny (the tyranny of sin) and now live in a Kingdom whose principles are based on the self-governing power of the Holy Ghost.

As we sit on that lovely hillside enjoying the thrill of the fireworks show, let's agree to say a prayer of thanksgiving to the Lord, our "founding father" whose Holy Word is our declaration of dependence on his lovingkindness.

Mercy Seat Message #159
"Communications vs. Communion"

In one of our Sunday Services, Elder Carol Madkins brought up the distinction between "communicating" and "communing" with God.

Communications, talking 'to' God, is great. It is the essence of prayer and the prerequisite for an intimate relationship with him. Obviously it's hard, as Carol pointed out, to get to know someone you don't talk to. As good as it is, communications is not as good as it gets.

Communing is being 'with' God...perhaps talking, often listening, regularly being silent in his awesome presence. That is the intimacy that he desires with you and I and the fellowship for which he saved us.

Take time to talk to him today. His ear, the Word says, is open to your cry. But more than that, <u>be</u> with him today. His arms are open wide to welcome you to sit with him upon his seat of mercy.

Mercy Seat Message #160
"Being A S.M.A.R.T. Christian"

One Sunday Pastor Rita ministered on being a "S.M.A.R.T." Christian. The acronym was helpful in keeping a focus on walking in victory with Christ.

S = "Selected"(1Peter 2:9) We belong to God and have received His calling. A smart Christian recognizes His claim to their lives.

M = "Mature" (1Peter 2:5) We know that we are nothing without Christ but are assured we can do all things if we rely on him as the source of our strength.

A = "Active" (1Peter 2:11) We can live as either refugees or royalty, sit on the sidelines or as a 'player' in the game, doing the will of God.

R = "Responsible" (1Peter 2: 13-17) If we honor all men, love the brethren, and fear God, we will possess the authority He has delegated to us.

T = "Trust" (1 Peter 2:21) Life is often not "fair" but neither are we doormats. Trusting him let's us know when it's time to claim one's rights and when to stand up for the rights of others.

Mercy Seat Message #161
"The Seasons of the Lord"

In preparing for a New Testament-style celebration of the Feast of Tabernacles you'll discover that the Jewish people have two calendars. One is to recognize the civil year, the other to keep track of the religious year.

Perhaps we should all recognize two calendars. One that governs our natural coming and going such as January to December, and another that is sensitive to the seasons of God's work of sanctification in our lives.

There is a perpetual 'Passover' where we are continually delivered from darkness, a perpetual 'Pentecost' where we allow the Holy Ghost to fill with us increasingly, and a perpetual 'Tabernacles' where the Lord is calling us to an even deeper relationship with Him.

Don't fight the seasons. Like the leaves on a tree yield to the coming of the Fall, yield your hearts to the seasons of the Lord.

Mercy Seat Message #162
"His Own Blood"

In the Fall, Jewish people celebrate their holiest day of their year—the Day of Atonement—when the High Priest made his once-a-year reconciliation of the sins of the people. He would enter the Holy of Holies, the third part of the Tabernacle of Moses, and sprinkle the blood of bulls and goats on the Ark of the Covenant.

We are told in Hebrews that Jesus, who is our High Priest, made a one-time offering of his own blood in God's tabernacle in the heavens, of which the one Moses made on earth was just a copy. This one-time offering forever cleansed our sins and set us free from a guilt-ridden conscience.

Those who celebrate this Day of Atonement will do so with somber penitence. They may still be waiting for their sins to be

<u>covered</u>. We, who are believers, can join in that celebration, but with a joyous freedom. With his own blood our sins have been <u>removed</u>.

Mercy Seat Message #163
"A Time to Turn"

The Jewish people's observance of the Day of Atonement (Yom Kippur) begins at sundown (like every day in the Biblical "calendar"). Yom Kippur is the final day of a 40-day season of "Teshuvah" or "repentance", being then the last opportunity to turn to God before the Feast of Ingathering (Tabernacles).

While it might be a stretch to connect world events with the timing of the Feasts, it is also foolish to overlook the reality of Biblical events. It is also foolish to overlook the fact that the Lord is always sending warnings of the need for you and I, unsaved people, and even nations, to turn to him and away from sinful ways.

If you ever heard the Lord compelling you to share the gospel, now might be the time. It is a time when many people who have never considered God are looking for him. It is a time for many when the questions are more numerous than the answers. It is a time of reckoning with their sense of safety and peace. It is a time to turn. It is the season of Teshuvah.

Mercy Seat Message #164
"An Open Door"

Although we as a country have been increasingly in the grip of tragedy the Lord is opening wide the door of reconciliation. The recent horrors of terrorism are driving many towards the beauty of holiness. People are asking about spiritual things......life, death, God, the devil.

God has a plan to save those who practice all forms of religion just as he has a plan for those who don't practice anything at all. The news media is broadcasting testimonies of faith, miracles, and hope in God as we listen to rescuers and survivors tell their stories.

The point is that the Lord is depending on you and I to answer those life and death questions, to share the plan he has, and to tell people who the real rescuer is. The next time someone raises the issues of politics or terrorists or threatening religious movements, don't debate. Open wide the door and show them the Way.

Mercy Seat Message #165
"The Eternal Connection"

Elder Pearlie Madkins shared a message in a continuing series on 'Renewing Your Mind'. She used the analogy of the reliability of the technology available to us today as a contrast with the steadfastness and faithfulness of the Lord.

For example, when you call on the name of the Lord of the Hosts:

—the server will never be down
—you'll never be put on hold
—your call will never be out of range
—the system will never lock up on you
—you will never be in a roaming area

We got the picture. We hope you get it to. Today, if at any point you need him, at any time you want to reach out to him, just call him up. The dialer lives within you. You have an 'eternal connection'.

Mercy Seat Message #166
"A New and Living Way"

Pastor Rita Thompson also shared a word in our "Renewing Your Mind" series. She reminded us of the Lord's work in bringing us to the fullness of the stature of the nature of Christ.

In our culture we are used to making an effort. We are prone to exerting whatever strength or leverage we have to accomplish a goal. But in Hebrews 10:16 we are told:

"This is the covenant that I will make with them after those days, saith the Lord, I will put my laws into their hearts, and in their minds will I write them."

The emphasis is on the "I". The "Lord" is making the covenant, and the "Lord" is doing the writing. As Pastor Rita reflected, 'you renew your mind by following after and believing God. To come into the presence of the living Lord in itself is to be changed."

Mercy Seat Message #167
"Dirty Diaper Love"

Elder Pearlie Madkins once gave us an encouraging reminder about God's love for us in a Sunday sermon. She used the analogy of a baby in dirty diapers to describe the unconditional love that our Father has for us.

Parents are never dismayed at their baby's dirty diapers. As unpleasant as it is, parents accept their responsibility to change dirty diapers as a normal part of their role. Dirty diapers never affect the love they have for their children, although the child certainly may not be happy with their "mess"!

When you and I make a mess, our Father is not necessarily happy about it either. But when He saved us he knew there would be times when he would have to change our dirty diapers. Our mess never affects the love he has for you, his child.

Mercy Seat Message #168
"Thank You For Giving to the Lord"

One Sunday we held a Day of Appreciation for our Elders, Pearlie Madkins and Carol Madkins. In honoring their service, one of our members offered the song, "Thank You for Giving to the Lord". It was a reminder and an encouragement to all of us as to who the object of any service must be.

It is easy in our individualistic culture for even believers to get sidetracked, and place too much emphasis on the reaction of people-who are usually the recipients of our giving. This often goes unrewarded and the giver soon grows weary, feels unappreciated and sometimes drifts into apathy.

If our giving is directed at him, from whom all blessings flow, we will always be refreshed and energized, no matter how few 'thank-yous' come our way. Remember what Jesus said..."what you have done for the least of them you have done unto me".

Mercy Seat Message #169
"How Much More Glorious?"

Pastor Rita was talking to me about the glory of God-that almost-tangible, life-changing "weight" that comes in the abundance of his presence. She used 2 Corinthians 3 to remind me of how the glory that the Lord has given us should affect those we have been given stewardship over.

When Moses returned from the mountain with the Law, the glory that covered him was so bright that others had to be shielded from it. 2 Corinthians 3 says that if the anointing of God was so great in the rules and regulations, how much more glorious is the anointing we possess of the Holy Ghost guiding and regulating us?

We can affect the lives of our family, friends and co-workers by exuding the glory that Jesus has given us. John 17 makes it clear that the gift of that glory must be imparted so that their lives too, will be changed into Jesus' image and likeness. Wherever you are today let that glory shine forth.

Mercy Seat Message #170
"When I See the Blood"

Paul tells us that the Old Testament was given to us as an example and a "schoolmaster to lead us to Christ". In the celebration of the Feast of Passover we see the miracle of salvation played out with the deliverance of the children of Israel from their Egyptian bondage.

Passover always reminds me of the power of the blood. In Exodus the Lord said that when he sees the blood that he directed them to put on the doorposts of their houses, that he would "pass over" them when he struck the land of Egypt with death. It didn't mean that a death wasn't required in that household, only that the slain lamb had taken the place of the death of the first-born person in that house.

Because that blood saves us, the evil one is prevented from "stealing, killing, and destroying". When the Lord sees the blood of Jesus on the 'doorposts' of your heart and mind, he will cause the destroyer to pass over you. The death of the first-born of many brethren, Jesus, has been accepted in your place.

Mercy Seat Message #171
"A Memorial Forever"

In Exodus the Lord gives his instructions for the observance of this feast of Passover. Among other things he tells the Israelites that it is to be a "perpetual feast", a "memorial forever". They are to always remember this time when the Lord led them out of the bondage of Egyptian captivity.

As Passover is a type of our salvation by the blood of Jesus, we would all do well to continually remember our escape from a life of sin. Our daily decisions, our battles against temptation, and our ability to hear the Lord's voice clearly, are all enhanced by the freshness of that memory.

There is great power in remembering. Today, whether you are behind a desk, a steering wheel, or a dishwasher, recall the day when your soul left Egypt. Recollect when the Red Sea of your wayward state was parted, and it was you, who walked on dry land. Remember your exodus from the kingdom of darkness and your entrance into the kingdom of his dear Son.

Mercy Seat Message #172
"Firstfruits"

When the children of Israel celebrated the Passover they were also instructed to observe the Feast of 'Firstfruits'. Eventually, upon arriving in the land of promise they were to take of the first shoots of their young wheat plants and present them to the Lord as an offering to be accepted by Him. They were told that the first born of everything belonged to the Lord, as He bestowed His blessing on the remainder.

What an amazing principle to incorporate into our lives today. If you find yourself getting angry, give him the "first part" of it and he will bless you with peace. If sadness or fear attempts to overtake you, give him the first part and he will bless you with joy and courage.

The celebration of the Feast of Firstfruits points us to the resurrection when Jesus, the "first-begotten of the dead" would rise from the grave. The offering of his life now making us acceptable to God.

Mercy Seat Message #173
"Be Converted"

Pastor Rita shared some profound insights from Acts 3 with me, when Peter and John met the beggar at the Gate Beautiful. After their encounter with him, Peter gave the crowd a history lesson on the coming of Jesus, ending with the call to "repent and be converted...". Every believer has understood the need to repent but what about being converted?

We are told that we have been "translated" from a fleshly existence where passions and desires direct our decisions, to a life where we let the Holy Ghost direct our path. Often people get saved but don't grow further in being converted.

When you share the saving grace of the Lord with others don't let them stop with just repenting because the real joy will be in their conversion. Ask them if..."Jesus is your Savior? Is He also your Lord? Are you co-laboring with Him to convert the filthy rags of your own goodness to the royal robes of His righteousness?"

Mercy Seat Message #174
"No Other Gods"

During a Sunday Praise and Worship, several prophetic words were shared, all emphasizing that there is only one God and none should be put before him. While none of us worships stone or wooden idols, do we really have other gods just the same?

The answer is an obvious 'yes', as many things get put before God and are given worship. Financial problems, health concerns, abuse in our past.... all can be put before the worship of the Lord.

The reminder we all received Sunday morning was not a harsh reprimand or a stinging rebuke. No, it was a firm and loving encouragement to consider that none of these other things in our life have any power when compared to the one, true, God. No problem exists for which he does not have the solution. No wilderness too rough that he cannot carve a path for you and I to walk through. No darkness too thick that the light of his love cannot chase away.

Mercy Seat Message #175
"Tithing-He Will Take Care Of You"

Elder Pearlie Madkins once gave an inspiring message that included a powerful reference to tithing. Many people in the body of Christ are automatically turned off to the very mention of it as the Church-at-large has put too much emphasis on money. In fact, the point Elder Madkins made was that it is not about money but about our relationship with the Lord.

The giving of the tenth part of our increase is a sign and a statement that we know him well enough to know that we can trust him to provide for us. We need not worry about the gleanings we have left in the fields, or that which we have dropped along the way.

I would encourage everyone who is not a tither to seek the Lord and ask for the revelation that the widow with only four mites to give must have had. She considered herself rich because she knew she had a relationship with him and that He would surely take care of her.

Mercy Seat Message #176
"A Formal Deposit"

In another of Elder Pearlie's Sunday messages on faith she made reference to "casting your cares" on the Lord. The definition she used for 'casting' was to make a 'formal deposit' of your cares.

Whenever you go to the bank to put money in your account, you make a formal deposit. After receiving a slip with the correct amount, most of us don't worry about whether our money is there. We take 'faith' that the bank will guard our hard earned income.

Today if you are facing problems or obstacles make a 'formal deposit'. Give it to the Lord and receive back the assurance that he will watch over your life. The good thing he has done in you, he promises to see it to completion. Cast your cares on him because he definitely cares for you.

Mercy Seat Message #177
"One Nation Under God"

You are probably all aware of the fact that our Pledge of Allegiance has been under attack because of the use of the phrase "under God." There are people who believe that it is unconstitutional to make reference to God. In fact, our Constitution has no such prohibition.

When separation of church and state was mentioned by our founding fathers, the context was protecting the Church from the State! They did not want the same thing that happened in England to happen here-for the State to dictate a particular Christian denomination as the country's religious faith.

We have removed reverence for God from our public schools and there are forces now at work to remove it from our loyalty to the principles of our nation. The same principles that guarantee everyone the right to worship God in whatever form or manner they choose. That freedom is ours because of his endowment. How long will we have freedom, if we fail to acknowledge the One who gave it to us?

Mercy Seat Message #178
"Whether You Know It Or Not"

A word of encouragement came forth one Sunday from a member of our fellowship, who had on her heart to remind us that the Lord is always with you, no matter how things may seem.

In the midst of trials and life's challenges, you can become convinced ourselves that the Lord is no longer near and can no longer hear your cry. As the Old Testament prophets expressed it, the 'sky can turn to brass'.

Don't let the enemy fool you. The Lord is always with you and always at work for you, even when it doesn't feel like it. 'He who keeps Israel neither slumbers nor sleeps'. He is moving your mountains and lifting up your valleys, whether you know it or not.

Mercy Seat Message #179
"Bearing Fruit"

At a workplace I talked about the difference between "fruit" and "seed". We have all been given the incorruptible seed of God's word and like anyone who plants, the Lord is expecting fruit.

One of the group gave this marvelous analogy. Imagine coming to someone's house for a picnic on a hot August day. The host offers you watermelon. The anticipation of tasting the cold, sweet, fruit is almost too much to bear. When the host returns, instead of that mouth-watering slice you expected to see, he deposits into your hand a pile of watermelon seeds!

'Fruit' is our character producing for those around us, the very life and nature of God. It is not enough to read and pray and study and praise. Those are all beautiful expressions of 'seed'. But what the world needs to see is what springs forth from our souls...fruit. They want to see Jesus.

Mercy Seat Message #180
"Thanks Giving Revisited"

We trust you are able to have the spirit of gluttony bound and enjoy your annual Thanksgivings. As believers we all know that as pleasant a reminder of our need to give thanks, for us is a full-time response-ability.

While we all probably acknowledge our thankfulness in our prayers, the Lord is looking for the action of our lives to be the real testimony of our thanks. The gratitude we feel for the Lord's blessings often remains inward, rather than becoming an expression of love to others.

If we are truly thankful then we should show it more. Do something thoughtful for a loved one. Better yet do something thoughtful for someone, like a co-worker, who you don't know very well. Or even better, do something thoughtful for someone you don't particularly get along with. You will see, and feel, the shower of his grace rain down in your life.

Mercy Seat Message #181
"Fall On Your Knees"

In the chorus to the popular Christmas song, "O Holy Night', it says to "fall on your knees and hear the angels voices..." When December dawns people will begin to get into full gear for Christmas. You and I know the 'reason for the season' and how often it can be lost in the hustle and bustle. It should be a time to remind ourselves of the awesome love of God in sending His Son, born to die for our sins.

The only real response to this great love is to fall on your knees. The Lord is worthy of our complete worship. He is to be honored, praised, adored, and given the glory that is due his name. Don't get lost in the hustle and bustle. Not just in the yule season, but right now, wherever you are today, at work or at home, take this moment to worship him, in spirit and in truth. Fall on your knees.

Mercy Seat Message #182
"Happy New You"

Everyone (who is up at that hour) wishes each other "Happy New Year " at the stroke of midnight on December 31. Next time around encourage each other to embrace the truth of 2 Corinthians 5:17 and wish ourselves a "Happy New You".

The magnitude of being a new creation in Christ can elude us of we aren't vigilant. When you were saved the Lord did not just fix what was broken, nor did he determine just to accept what was there. No, he re-created you in his image and likeness. And through the Holy Ghost gave you his life, his nature, and his power.

Whenever the enemy tries to bring out the worst in you, pause before you respond. Remind yourself that God has put his best in you. Remind yourself that the old things in you have passed away. Remind yourself that all things are new and all are of God. Then let the devil deal with that!

Mercy Seat Message #183
"Familiar Spirits"

Deuteronomy 18:10-12 provides a severe warning about seeking advice and direction from any source but God himself *"...There shall not be found among you any one that maketh his son or his daughter to pass through the fire, or that useth divination, or an observer of times, or an enchanter, or a witch, Or a charmer, or a consulter with familiar spirits, or a wizard, or a necromancer. For all that do these things are an abomination unto the LORD: and because of these abominations the LORD thy God doth drive them out from before thee."*

In a Sunday message on 'Familiar Spirits' Pastor Rita Thompson encouraged us to lean on the Lord for guidance and direction in all affairs of our lives. While most believers know that psychics and tarot cards are ungodly sources of advice, often we still don't take full advantage of our access to the Holy Ghost.

When you come to that crossroad today-whether it is a big or little decision,—lean not on your own understanding. Trust the

Lord to give you direction. His word is a lamp unto your feet and a light unto your path.

Mercy Seat Message #184
"He Will Fight For You"

Each spring as the Passover season approaches we are reminded of the story of the exodus of the children of Israel from Egypt. More than anything we are reminded of God's hand in their deliverance. Knowing that the Passover symbolizes the sacrifice of Jesus on the cross to release us from the bondage of sin, we are reminded as well, of God's hand in our own deliverance.

When the Israelites were being pursued by the army of Pharaoh, they found themselves backed up against the Red Sea. God's word to them was "stand still and see the salvation of the Lord". The Lord himself broke the wheels off the Egyptian chariots giving the Israelites the opportunity to escape. We know the rest of the story...

Today you may be pursued by your enemies and seemingly have no place to turn. Rest assured that as you call on his name, he will not address your situation 'long distance'. No, the Lord is always present. He, himself, will be your deliverer. The Lord himself will fight for you.

Mercy Seat Message #185
"Pentecost Promise"

You are undoubtedly familiar with the passages in Exodus where the Ten Commandments are delivered. There is an important moment in those passages where it says that the Lord himself appeared before them and the children of Israel promise to "do all that has been spoken".

Of course they experienced great difficulty in keeping that promise. For us, however, the power of Pentecost is that we can keep it, having received the Holy Ghost. The Holy Ghost is living in us, leading, guiding, and empowering us to behave in obedience to God's law.

It is no longer a question of whether you are strong enough to resist sinful impulses. It is only a matter of whether you are willing to choose to allow him to resist through you. God is the lawgiver and the Holy Ghost at Pentecost now becomes your law-keeper.

Mercy Seat Message #186
"Keep Yourself"

Jude 20 tells us to keep ourselves "in the love of God". In one of her Sunday messages Elder Pearlie Madkins encouraged us to take this scripture to heart, understanding that we can take ourselves "out of" the love of God if we allow it.

From her perspective, much of our ability to "stay" in the love of God boils down to what we perceive to be our reward. If the reward of salvation and the kingdom of God is what it can do for you, then your love relationship with the Lord can be challenged by circumstances and life's situations. On the other hand, if you see the person of Jesus <u>as the reward</u>, it strengthens your spiritual resolve.

The intimacy of knowing him <u>is</u> the gift of salvation. The right of access to his grace and complete acceptance by him as his child eclipses all earthly benefits. Yes, the Lord will bless your natural affairs and prosper the works of your hands. But the greatest reward is to be embraced by his glory and to be kept in His love.

Mercy Seat Message #187
"The Power of Joy"

Elder Carol Madkins wrapped up our series on Romans 14:17 ("*For the kingdom of God is not meat and drink; but righteousness, and peace, and joy in the Holy Ghost.*") by sharing a message on joy. Unlike 'happiness', joy has an enduring quality over and above the circumstances we may face.

Happiness is good......agreed? But like the weather, this condition can change at a moment's notice and is an unreliable indicator of reality. Happiness can be based on either the truth or a lie and it's hard not to chase after the good feelings that embody it. However, when times get tough, happiness loses its power.

Joy is that deep and comforting knowledge that God always has your "best interests at heart". As we grow wiser we begin to understand that things may not look and feel that way, but that knowledge has real power in helping us confirm the presence of His unchanging hand. Be happy? Absolutely. Tap into the joy that is in the Holy Ghost? Essential.

Mercy Seat Message #188
"It's Time For Tabernacles"

When fall looms It's that season again! No, not football, Tabernacles! The Feast season described in Leviticus 23:23, incorporates some of the most awesome references to the person and presence of Jesus in the Old Testament you will find. In fact, the Jewish people still refer to the period from the 'Trumpets' and 'The Day of Atonement ' as 'The Days of Awe'.

As New Testament believers it is the awesome picture of Jesus that we focus on and celebrate. Jesus' voice is echoed and his coming is announced at "Trumpets". When the Old Testament High Priest entered the Holy of Holies and sprinkled the blood of the sacrifice on that mercy seat, it was depicting Jesus as our High Priest pouring His own blood in the mercy seat in heaven. (See Hebrews 9-13). He is the Succoth (booth) that is constructed as your dwelling place.

When season approaches prepare your heart to celebrate the Feast. It's irrelevant whether it is an outward celebration or simply the inward acknowledgement of the power of the symbols and their meaning in your life in the person of the Lord. Drink in the beauty of Psalms 89:15-18, a scripture traditionally read at Tabernacles: *"Blessed is the people that know the joyful sound* (of the Trumpet): *they shall walk, O LORD, in the light of thy countenance. In thy name shall they rejoice all the day: and in thy righteousness shall they be exalted. For thou art the glory of their strength: and in thy favour our horn shall be exalted."*

Mercy Seat Message #189
"Election Days-Doing Our Part"

At election times, millions of us will go the polls and cast our votes for candidates who are running for office at all levels. The media is saturated with lots of issues to consider. War in Iraq, health care, abortion, traditional marriage definition, stem cell research.... The list is not endless but sometimes it really does seem like it.

The issues are important. None of us should be ignorant of what someone running for Congress, State Representative or President stands for, and what the implications of their decisions could be. At the same time however, it's not the issues that ultimately will direct our hands to pull a particular lever or touch a name on a screen. We have to know that the Lord has a plan for our district, our state, and our nation, such that he has ordered the course of events to complete that plan. It is important therefore for each of us to ask him who to cast <u>our</u> vote for.

There have been "good" Pharaohs and "bad" Pharaohs, "good" Kings and "bad" Kings, and the Lord has used them all. No matter whether your choice is the "good" King who lost or the "bad" King who won, we are commanded by the scriptures to pray for those who are in authority and to submit cheerfully to their place in our government. If we obey the Lord we will be doing our part to bring forth his perfect will and purpose. We will be doing our part in the unfolding of his plan.

Mercy Seat Message #190
"Presents Or His Presence"

When the Christmas season is in full bloom many people's attention is naturally turned to the birth of the Savior. Many others' attention is focused on gifts, gadgets, and what they may get under a tree. This is a marvelous opportunity for those of us who know the Giver of all gifts, and the most precious gift he ever gave, his only begotten Son who hung on a different kind of tree.

Being able to enter into the very presence of God, just as we are, is an incredible thing. Not only will he accept us because of Jesus' sacrifice, but Almighty God desires our fellowship. Nothing that is sad, weak, or broken can stay that way in his presence. Everything is transformed by his magnificent glory. That glory is the feeling of peace, assurance, and comfort that you find when you put aside your cares and worries to listen to his voice.

This will be more than just "good" news to your friends, family, co-workers, and neighbors who don't know him. As joyous as the holiday season is for some, it is equally painful and depressing for others. It will be "great" news to those who are hurting, that there is much more to Christmas than just presents. His presence may be just what they need to find under the tree.

Mercy Seat Message #191
"The Third Well"

Rev. Sam Greene from Narrow Way Ministries in Jacksonville FL is a beloved brother and prophet to our church. He loves to share a message of encouragement on the body of Christ pressing in to a place of unity and blessing.

In Genesis 26 Isaac digs two wells that spring up with living water. But each time strife and discord spring up faster than the water. But Isaac presses on and digs a third well and finally there was harmony among the brethren " ...and he called the name of it Rehoboth; and he said, For now the LORD hath made room for us, and we shall be fruitful in the land."

If you read on in Genesis 26 you will see there was a fourth well which causes even the people who do not know the Lord to come to that place to drink. In these days when the world is thirsty for living water, we need to flee from strife and discord as believers. We need to reach that "third well" where each of our gifts and insights, regardless of denomination or group, allow us to become that many-membered" body that all creation is waiting for. When we do that, the world will know us by our love for another and they flock to our churches to drink.

Mercy Seat Message #192
"We Are The Branches"

In a Sunday message on "Character", Elder Carol Madkins once reminded us of the scripture in John 15 where Jesus says that "...*I am the vine, ye are the branches: He that abideth in me, and I in him, the same bringeth forth much fruit: for without me ye can do nothing.* " She emphasized the importance of bearing fruit and our obligation to the Lord to walk in a level of obedience that allows fruit to come forth from our life. Often the process of developing the character to be trusted with fruit is not easy.

Whether trials and tribulations enter our lives because of our shortcomings, the devil's strategies, or God's sovereignty, the Lord uses all of them to develop our character. How you respond to the difficulties of life will make the difference in your being ready and able to bear fruit for the kingdom of God. As our founding pastor, Cameron Simmons, used to tell us: you never know what is in the toothpaste tube until you put the squeeze on!

He is the vine and we are the branches. The fruit that we produce brings glory to the vine and the branch cannot take credit for it. All the branch can do is respond in obedience to the direction of the branch. It can receive the nourishment from the branch and use the wind, rain, snow, heat, darkness, and light-whatever comes it's way- to bring forth fruit. Allow the Lord to develop his character in you so you will not only be fruitful, but walk in the abundance of your fruit-bearing.

Mercy Seat Message #193
"For God So Loved"

Every February 14 bouquets of roses, candy hearts, and decorative valentine cards will be given to loved ones. Romantic gestures and special attention to the demonstration of our commitments will abound. It is the time of the year when the sentiment of love is freely expressed and encouraged. It is a time when love is remembered and celebrated.

The Bible speaks of different kinds of love. There is romantic love (eros) and the love between friends and family (filial). They are both good, and warm the heart when they are shared. But there is a love that extends beyond these-it is agape, a self-sacrificing, covenant love. Agape is the love that God had for us when he, as John 3:16 describes, "...gave his only begotten Son, that whosoever believeth in him should not perish, but have everlasting life."

Agape love is the only love that will never disappoint you, fail you, leave you, forsake you, or let you down. It will be yours regardless of what you do, or don't do, to deserve it. It will love you the most when you are the most unlovable. It is the love of which God himself has guaranteed by his own blood.

Mercy Seat Message #194
"Purity From The Inside Out"

When Elder Carol Madkins shares her message on "Purity" she always raises a critical point in understanding the ways of the Lord. We live in an "outside-in" world that focuses mainly on that which is external as a guide to gauging that which is internal. For example, we look at a person's dress, appearance, skin color or demeanor, to determine whom they are rather than the content of their character as a person.

But we serve a Lord who is an 'inside-out' God. He works <u>in</u> us to affect changes in our <u>inner being</u> that will eventually manifest themselves in our external actions. He looks at a person's heart to determine who and what they are, knowing that it is a better reflection of reality than just that which can be seen.

If you are struggling with issues in your life seek the Lord for help in changing what is going on in your heart and mind. If you get a revelation of purity on the inside it will begin to manifest itself on the outside. Don't get fooled into looking outside of yourself for the answers to questions in your life. Inside you dwells the Spirit of God, whose job it is to lead and guide you into all truth.

Mercy Seat Message #195
"A Royal Priesthood"

More good teaching from the Pentagon Women's Bible Study...Pastor Derrell Emerson of Christian Assembly talked about our "priesthood" as believers in Jesus. 1 Peter 2: 9 tells us "But ye are a chosen generation, a royal priesthood, an holy nation, a peculiar people; that ye should show forth the praises of him who hath called you out of darkness into his marvellous light." Our priesthood extends to God for man and to man from God.

We are called to be the point of contact for the grace of God in all the earth. Just as the Hebrew High Priest was the only one to enter into the Holy of Holies on behalf of the sins of the people of Israel, we believers are welcomed into the presence of Almighty God as intercessors for his will in the lives of all people.

As a holy priesthood we also occupy the distinctive responsibility of bringing God's will to men and women. We may be the only time many hear the "voice of God" as we proclaim his truth to a sick and dying world.

Like the Levites our portion comes directly from the Lord and we belong to him. We are indeed a holy nation and a peculiar people. 'Peculiar' does mean strange, however. It means a people of "great value" as instruments in the hand of a loving God.

Mercy Seat Message #196
"Unleavened Bread"

When Jesus and His disciples gathered to celebrate the Passover, it was the beginning of the Feast of Unleavened Bread. When Moses led the children of Israel out of Egyptian bondage they were commanded to not only eat the Passover lamb in haste, but, for seven days following, to eat nothing but unleavened bread- bread baked also in such haste that the dough did not have time to rise. This was to be in commemoration of their freedom. To us, it is also a powerful message about the satisfying power of salvation.

Leaven is symbolic of sin. In Jewish homes all over the world, a ceremony of going through the house and removing any trace of leaven will be performed at that time. This ceremony symbolizes the removal of our sinful nature and a command to live in the holiness that has been purchased for us. As Paul said in both Corinthians and Galatians, "a little leaven leavens the whole lump".

It is sometimes difficult to keep the leaven out. We are bombarded from so many different directions and can get overwhelmed by temptation. Instead of feeling condemned and wallowing in shame, we need to seize the power of Jesus, who is the unleavened bread. When you are on the verge of falling, even when you begin to feel your mind drift towards the leaven, just call on his name and ask for help. You will never, ever, ever, find yourself in a position where, when you really want to get out the leaven, that he will not be there. He will not just make you strong so you can resist. He will be strong through you. He cannot only bolster your will so that you can say no. He can also remove that which you are confronting far from you.

Mercy Seat Message #197
"Lift Jesus Higher"

In a Sunday message, Elder Pearlie Madkins once shared an encouraging word about the preeminence of Jesus in God's plan of redemption. Unlike all other faiths, this Redeemer took the form of those who were to be redeemed. Our sinful nature incurred a debt to God, which could only be paid through our death, as breakers of his law. Jesus removed the bondage of our sinful nature by tasting of the death that belongs to that nature so that you and I would be released. Christians are called to be salt and light in a world badly in need of that same redemption.

Many people call on 'God' when they are in trouble or distress. Many people feel the burden of their sinful nature and do lots of good works in an attempt to gain redemption. But without the access to God that Jesus' death on the cross provides, there is no access. There is only the depth of God's grace that can spare them of temporary evils and events and only the accepting of that sacrifice can save them eternally.

We are told in Hebrews 4:16 "Let us therefore come boldly unto the throne of grace, that we may obtain mercy, and find grace to help in time of need". We can come boldly because Jesus has made it possible for us to appear in God's presence undefiled and seen as sinless. Let us continue to use that access to plead for those who do not know Jesus to come to the light and taste of the salt.

Mercy Seat Message #198
"In His Image And Likeness"

Elder Carol Madkins loves to recall events during her childhood when she shares the word. I remember when she was talked about growing and being repeatedly told that she looked "just like her father". As a young girl this did not seem like the glowing compliment it was intended to be. But as she grew older, and saw what a respected and honorable man her father was, it indeed became a compliment.

When she made the connection to God the Father, it made us all think about whether people would say that, we too, looked just like our Father, and how we need to get to know Him even better. We are made in His image and likeness, and though this clearly does not refer to our physical appearance, people really should be able to see His reflection in our words and deeds.

On the day when we recognize the blessings of our earthly fathers, Elder Carol helped us all to see our heavenly father more clearly. His love, compassion, and ever-present care for us needs to be recognized daily. We pray that as you spend time with Him, getting to know Him better, His image and likeness will be seen through you, too.

Mercy Seat Message #199
"His Name In Vain"

Elder Carol Madkins does a great job of articulating the meaning of the 3rd Commandment....it means exactly what it says! That meaning is simply for us to not speak vain (empty) words, in any capacity or form. Naturally profanity is a bad thing but it goes far beyond that. According to Carol (and to the Bible, by the way) we are the Lord's ambassadors here in the earth. We represent the attributes of God, his character and the qualities of his kingdom.

To say anything that is without merit, value, or positiveness, is an empty (vain) word. As his representatives, as those who reflect those attributes, that emptiness is an affront to who he is. It is an affront to his name. That's lot to live up to, I know. But Elder Carol was not finished....A "euphemism" is when you substitute a vague term for something more harsh or specific. It's like when instead of speaking a profane word, we say "Gosh" or "Darn" or "Shucks". It's a lot to handle, but such euphemisms are just as "vain" as the bad words they stand for, simply because it was the thought in our minds that produced the need for the word.

Wow, I don't know about you, but at the Global Truth Ministries we are realizing the need for a whole new level of holiness. Not just managing what comes out of our mouths, but as Jesus said, seeking holiness for the abundance of the heart from which the mouth speaks. We want that holiness and are willing to watch our words. We want to obey God and have determined to keep quiet altogether, if that's what it takes to not take that precious name in vain.

Mercy Seat Message #200
"The Need"

When Elder Pearlie Madkins shared her message on taking faith for holiness, she talked about how the Lord works the need for a sin out of our hearts. It seems that most sin is based on "need".

In other words, we wrongly choose things and thoughts to satisfy a lack, a craving, or a desire of our fleshly nature. The sin is not just the thing or the thought, but even more so, our failure to let the Lord fill the need.

Remember, John the Baptist said that the "axe has been laid to the root of the tree." Among other things, he seemed to be making reference to the fact that with the coming of Messiah that fundamental waywardness in humanity would be taken care of. In your life today what is the need that any sin is trying to fulfill? If you can answer that question then just ask the Lord to fill it. He will lay the axe to the root and remove the need for anything but him.

Mercy Seat Message #201
"Rosh Hashanah "

When we get to the Feast of Trumpet, it is the announcement of the beginning of the New Year (Rosh Hashanah) and a call to prepare yourself for the Yom Kippur (Day of Atonement).

For us as believers there is also a trumpet sounding in that season. It is the announcement that each day in the Lord can also be a new year, a new season, a new beginning for anyone who needs one. It is also a call to us believers to prepare for a new level of personal holiness in our daily lives. Grace is great but it does not mean that we should not bring an offering of sacrifice to the Lord. Grace does not mean that we are through putting to death our old nature with its lusts and depravities. It means we need to make increasingly better choices as we are free from the need to sin.

We are told to not appear before the Lord on a feast day empty-handed. There is a trumpet sounding in your life to bring those sinful habits and thought patterns before the Lord so that the blood can be applied to them and cleanse your mind and heart. Hear the trumpet sounding in your life and bring him your weakness, your frailty, and your need for anything but him.

Mercy Seat Message #202
"Fire By Night"

"Succoth" or the Feast of Booths is a precious time of celebration. For this feast, as part of the Feast Of Tabernacles, the Jewish people were told to build a booth as a reminder of the temporary shelter the Lord provided for them in their 40 years in the wilderness. During that time he made sure they were cared for in every way as they journeyed.

We too can have episodes in the 'wilderness'. Life's calamites, and those periods of time when the Lord is stretching us to reach for a new level of holiness and relationship with him, can feel like being in the wilderness. And herein lies the powerful message to us about this Feast.... he is there with you!

Yep. In their wilderness, he also had them build him a temporary place to dwell, and stayed with them every step of the way, until they crossed over into the Land of Promise. You need to know today that he is with you in your wilderness. He is not standing on the outside watching you deal with circumstances. No, he is right there in the midst of them with you. When things get tight do what he told the Jewish people to do. Look for the cloud of His glory during the day and the fire by night.

Mercy Seat Message #203
"Be Ye Separate"

I love it when the youngsters at church get a chance to share. One of our really precious ones, Lesley Davis, shed light on an important aspect of being a minister of reconciliation during. By the way, Lesley was a 13-year-old high school student at the time, but her understanding of holiness, and living a life consecrated to God, was full-grown. She made the meaning of 'in the world but not of the world' as clear as it can get. We are to refuse to imitate the way the world does things, but at the same time, we must be available for those lost in darkness.

She referenced 2 Corinthians 6:14-17 *(Be ye not unequally yoked together with unbelievers: for what fellowship hath righteousness with unrighteousness? and what communion hath light with darkness? And what concord hath Christ with Belial? or what part hath he that believeth with an infidel? And what agreement hath the temple of God with idols? for ye are the temple of the living God; as God hath said, I will dwell in them, and walk in them; and I will be their God, and they shall be my people. Wherefore come out from among them, and be ye separate,).*

In our community, in our workplace, nearly everywhere we travel, we will encounter the pressure to conform. We will constantly, and consistently, be barraged to act, talk, dress, and even eat, the way everyone else does, just for the sake of fitting in. But Christians don't fit in. We don't have to 'belong' because we are just passing through. We are here for a short time to allow the life of Jesus to be lived through us to minister to other people. Think, if a 13-year-old can comprehend this and live it in the pressure of her peers, we all can do it. Be available to everyone who crosses your path. But in your habits, thoughts, and behaviors, come out from among them and be ye separate.

Mercy Seat Message #204
"Prepare Ye The Way"

Paul and Mary Birt, of Victorious Living Ministries, sound a wake-up call to the church, on what we need to be about in these last days. Every believer knows that Jesus is coming back. We may, however, have different perspectives on the how and why of His return. Certainly there is room in the body of Christ for a variety of viewpoints, on issues that are not at the core of what it means to be a disciple of the Lord Jesus Christ. At the same time, it is important that we all recognize what the Bible says about even these types of issues.

We know for example, that the church he is coming back for is without spot (moral blemish), wrinkle (divisive issues), or blemish (faultless before God). We know that it is a glorious church (held in great esteem). Even these few characteristics present a significant challenge for us as individuals, let alone for the myriad groups that comprise this body. But there are those of us who now hear the voice of the Bride, and are ready to respond to that challenge.

We need to have unity. We have to be willing to let our perspectives take a back seat to embracing each other as believers. We simply cannot let our view of the rapture, tongues, how you baptize people, what day the Sabbath is, whether women can wear makeup....or anything from the long list of issues that keep us apart as the people of God. Take the challenge. Reach out to fellow believers, not based on their church's statement of faith, but by the blood that saved you both. Come together as the bride and prepare the way of the Lord.

Mercy Seat Message #205
"Thou Shalt Do No Murder"

Elder Carol Madkins truly provides a thorough exegesis of the sixth commandment. Outside of clarifying the many issues that this commandment touches upon, she can take your understanding to another level. That level was the same one that Jesus took the Pharisees to in Matthew 5:21-22, " *Ye have heard that it was said by them of old time, Thou shalt not kill; and whosoever shall kill shall be in danger of the judgment: But I say unto you, That whosoever is angry with his brother without a cause shall be in danger of the judgment:...".*

Jesus was trying to help them see that what you harbor in your heart, as Carol said, is the real problem. Though you may not actually commit the act of murder, hatred and evil intent towards another person is the same. Why? Because the act is simply the manifestation of the thought. And in the kingdom of God it is purity of heart and holiness of mind that God is looking at. We all will have numerous chances to see exactly what is in our hearts today.

If you travel the highway, work in a pressurized environment, or have to tend to the hectic schedule of family life, your heart attitude will be tested. The key will not be how strong you can be or how much will power you have. The key will be, as Elder Carol demonstrated, how quickly and easily you allow Jesus to be who he is through you in those situations. If <u>you</u> respond, the outcome is generally predictable. Even the most intensive biting-of-the-lip and holding of the breath will soon give way. If you allow Jesus to manifest himself through you the outcome is equally predictable. Peace will prevail and the love of God will enlarge all it touches.

Mercy Seat Message #206
"We Wish You A Merry Christmas?"

There are forces at work in our culture will eventually make even the idea of Christmas itself a subject of constitutional debate. It will become increasingly questionable to impose your beliefs on other people, especially if they are Christian beliefs. Take heart though.

The scriptures make it clear that such times will come, and rather than being a sign of things getting "worse", they are actually the signs of the rising up of righteousness. You see, the Bible tells us that when sin abounds, grace abounds even further. So the darker things become and the more pressure the church is placed under, the more you can be assured that grace is bombarding the realms of darkness to an even greater extent.

Know for sure that days of persecution are coming. This is not a negative point of view. It's just what the scriptures seem to be saying. God's day always begins in the darkness. As the grip of our culture seems to tighten around the church, know for sure that it is only a sign that the time of our arising grows near.

Part IV

POWER IN THE PROMISES

I f you comprehend the full measure of your righteousness then you'll also comprehend that the promises that the Lord has made for your life must come to pass. As the scriptures suggest, to break his promise to you would be to deny himself. Why? Because, the Lord promised "himself" that he would bless you! Ultimately the power in his promises is the extent to which they have become real on the inside of you, way down deep inside your mind, your emotions, and your sense of who you are. It is not just about what you say or even what you think on a conscious level but what you really believe at the level of your self-talk.

If the little voice inside your head condemns you as being worthless and undeserving, then the word of the Lord has not yet penetrated far enough into your psyche. It is the price of the cross that has now made you worthy and deserving. If the little voice confirms this and the whole of what the scriptures say is true about you, then his promises will be real. We sometimes forget that the Lord has done "all" he intends to do for us. If we can embrace our righteousness thereby seeking first the kingdom of God, then, yes, all these things will be added to us.

Mercy Seat Message #207
"He Inhabits the Praises"

I find it necessary to regularly remind myself of the reality of God's promises and the tangible power of the Word of God. Yeah, we all 'know' that he supposedly "inhabits the praises of his people", but when do we exercise that truth? Sunday morning is an obvious opportunity and a wonderful time to experience the corporate joy of his inhabitation. But what about other times?

You've just been told you'll have to work the weekend. Will the frustration of the news leave you empty and angered or can you allow him to inhabit some praises? The fridge breaks down and the little money you did have saved for a rainy day is now washed away. Will you give him a chance to inhabit some praises?

The point is that it's easy for his inhabitation to happen on Sunday. But is that when you'll really, really need the power of his presence? The anointing of God is available for us in times of stress and times of trouble. Practice praising him so you will be inclined to call on him when it counts the most.

Mercy Seat Message #208
"The Depth Of His Love"

With the pressures of our culture and the pace of our lives it can be easy to forget the depth of God's love and concern for us. We often think that we are simply one of many that God loves rather than remembering his ability to love billions of us one at a time as if we were the only one.

Psalm 139 provides a strong reminder of the personal nature of God's love for you. It says things like "He has searched you and knows you", and that he understands your every thought and is with you in your every movement throughout your day. Nothing you say today comes forth without his inspiration and there is nowhere you will end up today where he will not be present with you. God has known and loved you for a long time-even when you were still in your mommy's tummy. He knew then that you had faults and shortcomings and loved you all the more for them.

As the Psalmist says, upon reflection of God's love for you, you will discover that you cannot count the good thoughts he has of you. Try anyway.

Mercy Seat Message #209
"I Know the Plans..."

Imagine being led on a tour of a museum, historical site, or other venue by a guide with years and years of experience in walking people through the wonders of the location. Imagine at every stop you interrupt the guide and question: "...where are we going next???" "are you really sure you know how to get us there???", "do you really know what you're talking about?", "how much longer until we're at the end of the tour?" and on and on.

If you're starting to think that you and I are sometimes that nervous person on the tour, continually questioning the Holy Ghost (our tour guide in this life) you're getting the point. Jeremiah 29:11 says, *"For I know the thoughts that I think toward you, saith the Lord, thoughts of peace and not of evil, to give you an expected end."* Just as the pillar of smoke and the column of fire led the children of Israel, the Holy Ghost knows the way out of our personal wilderness. Instead of questioning so much we need to trust the tour guide more. He's been leading people on this since eternity, and no one has ever been disappointed or asked for their money back.

Mercy Seat Message #210
"An Everlasting Love..."

If you've been a Bible reader for any length of time you know from the Word that the Lord has an "everlasting love" for us, he will "never leave or forsake us". we are the "apple of his eye"... and so on. But have we really begun to comprehend what it really means? This kind of love is not the same as the love of the best Mom or Dad in the world, who will love their children no matter what. As good as that love is you could create a scenario where even the deepest of human love would wane or diminish.

But this love that God has for you knows no condition. There is no circumstance you can dream up where he would decide not to love you. That is almost impossible for the human mind to understand. It runs counter to what we have learned about love-it must be earned and will be retracted if we fail to perform our part. Even in the worst of the judgments against Israel God never withdrew his love. No matter how rebellious or intentionally disobedient we behave he will never withdraw his love. The gospel says that because of that great love our hearts are then moved to obedience, faith, and trust. At some point in your hectic day stop and let God love you.

Mercy Seat Message #211
"The Blood Will Never Lose Its Power"

In churches all over the world, Sunday services include either songs about the blood of Jesus, the partaking of communion where the wine represents that precious blood, or other expressions relating to the shed blood of the Lamb of God. In our service we sometimes sing the chorus that says, "the blood will never lose its power".

As you think about the meaning of the blood of Jesus, the eternal freshness of it, and its unending power to cleanse, your heart should well up with a majestic peace. Knowing that none of your sins, infirmities or weaknesses can extend beyond the grip of God's grace should bring you an astounding sense of comfort.

It means literally that you will always be precious in his sight. He will always receive you with the same honor that he receives the Son. Because of the blood, you have been made the righteousness of God in Christ Jesus.

Critics of our beliefs have looked to the almost endless sacrifice of animals in the Old Testament and the cruel sufferings of Jesus on the cross and denigrated Christianity as a "bloody religion". It takes a revelation of who God is indeed to grasp the message behind such carnage. When you do your only response will be: "Thank God for the blood".

Mercy Seat Message #212
"A Time for Miracles"

If you read through the Gospels you will notice an interesting pattern. Whenever Jesus wanted to direct people's attention to the presence of God he worked miracles and/or miraculous healings. These actions were never to draw attention to himself, or done just for the sake of doing something spectacular. He always had a spiritual purpose in demonstrating that power and presence.

There has never been a time in human history when mankind had more things to distract us from the presence of God. Gadgets, technology, a wealth of diversions...all easily get in the way of acknowledging Him. It is time for us who are called by his name to seek the gifts of God in order to draw attention to him.

I'm not suggesting thrill seeking or being caught up with experiences-I think the church has had enough of that in the last 100 years or so. No, I'm talking about the real thing-Holy Ghost-guided, God-birthed, salvation-inspiring signs and wonders.

The fact that this probably sounds silly to many is further evidence of how far we have strayed from the clear message of the Bible. In Luke 9, as in many other places, "He called the twelve disciples together, and gave them power and authority over all devils, and to cure diseases. And he sent them to preach the kingdom of God, and to heal the sick."

Let's seek him for the gifting to proclaim his Word and unleash his Power. If he is lifted up all men will be drawn to him. Now is the time for miracles.

Mercy Seat Message #213
"Delegated Authority"

We are told in 2 Corinthians 5 that we are "ambassadors" for Christ. This subtle pronouncement is full of invigorating insight.

For one, an ambassador represents a foreign country. He or she is not native to the country that they have been called to be ambassadors to, just as we are not native to this earth. We have been given a spiritual birth and owe our allegiance to a spiritual home-the dwelling place of God. We are as Abraham, "travelers", but unlike

Abraham we have found our true home-heaven-a place that awaits us when our travels are completed and our mission fulfilled.

Ambassadors come in the full authority of the one who sent them. Their word carries the full weight and power of the one who sent them, provided they have been given the word to be spoken. The authority that Jesus has delegated to us is not to be used at our whim, but in light of what the Spirit and the Word of God have spoken to us.

An ambassador carries out the will of the higher authority rather than make up his or her own mind about what should take place. It is incumbent upon ambassadors to find out the will of the one who has sent them. We must spend time with the King to know what is on his heart.

Fulfill your role as an ambassador for Christ. Get the instructions and operate in his authority to carry them out.

Mercy Seat Message #214
"Take Diligent Heed"

Joshua 22 tells us to"...take _diligent_ _heed_ to do the commandment and the law, which Moses the servant of the LORD charged you, to love the LORD your God, and to walk in all his ways, and to keep his commandments, and to cleave unto him, and to serve him with all your heart and with all your soul."

This quality of diligence is important to us receiving all that the Lord has for us. The scripture essentially tells us to take "great pains" (diligent heed) to love, walk, keep, cleave, and serve. If we are faithful to do our part we will see increasing blessings of the Lord, as he is always faithful to do his part.

Don't let the passivity of the world around you lull you into inactivity. The kingdom of God still suffers violence and the violent still take it by force. At the same time, don't let our works-oriented culture deceive you into thinking that it is by your own strength that you seize the kingdom. Certainly don't let it make you think that your salvation hinges on those works either.

Christ in you is the hope of glory and he will be strong on your behalf if you just let him love you.

Mercy Seat Message #215
"The Gift of Grace"

We all have experienced "grace" but often cannot really define it in order to communicate to new believers or those curious about the things of God. Grace is the key ingredient of life in the kingdom of God and the true distinguishing factor between faith in Jesus the Christ and other "faiths". Grace is God's decision to love us "to death".

God deals with us by loving us even before we knew who he was. He poured his love out on us at the cross and continues to love us as he sanctifies us in our walk with him. He loves us despite our tendency towards disobedience and rebellion. He loves us in the midst of our worst days without condition. He loves us with such passion that at some point we are overcome with love.

Once overcome we determine to obey and then even to "die" to the things that hold us back from a deeper love for God. We submit to the authority of God because of his great love for us renders us incapable of any other response. Grace is love we do not deserve but which God has decided that we are worthy of because of the blood of the Lamb.

Mercy Seat Message #216
"Tire-Jack Religion"

All of us know what a tire jack is. It's the thing you keep somewhere in the trunk of your car, buried under various debris. You never pay any attention to it on a regular basis.

But at that fateful moment, usually on some dark rainy highway, you hear and then feel, your tire go flat. At that moment as you search frantically through the trunk, that tire jack is the most valuable possession you own.

Once it's done its work and you're out of a jam you throw it back in the trunk until the next time you get into tire trouble.

Don't ever let your relationship with God become a 'tire-jack religion". Don't just call on him when you get in a jam, knowing he'll be there to get you out of it. Once you're delivered he goes back with the rest of the debris of your mind and heart.

Keep him on the front seat next to you. In fact give him the steering wheel and let Him choose your direction. Keep him first place in your life and just may never need your "tire-jack religion".

Mercy Seat Message #217
"DownPayment on Things to Come"

The Apostle Paul refers to the presence of the Holy Ghost in you as the "earnest" of our inheritance. Just as when you buy a house you place a deposit with the lender to hold the house for you until the papers are signed. The deposit is not the house, nor does it allow you to really enjoy any of the features of the house.

As wonderful as it might be to have the peace, power, and confidence in God because of the Holy Ghost living in you, it does not compare to what we will enjoy when the glory of God is revealed in us in its fullness.

It's important for us to remember this. Lots of things come our way in this life and without the knowledge that there is something unbelievably wonderful awaiting us, one could easily despair. But Paul reminds us that the "sufferings of this present time" don't compare either, to the glory to come.

Don't live today waiting for tomorrow. Enjoy what it brings with it. But don't be discouraged if things aren't going so well. There are incredibly better days ahead.

Mercy Seat Message #218
"Setting Your Affections"

It's amazing sometimes when you consider how little the Lord really asks of you, versus what he is willing to do through you. In Colossians 3:2 it says to simply *"Set your affections on things above, not on things of the earth".* To 'set your affections' means to exercise your mind, entertain or have a sentiment or strong opinion. In this case, a strong opinion about heavenly things, eternal things, and not the perishable, temporary qualities of this world we "live" in.

The results of these thoughts are profound indeed. If you read further it implies that you will become dead to the unfruitful emotions, passions, and desires that sin can produce in your life. Of course it's not without making some quality decisions. But the starting point for deliverance is so simple---formulate a strong opinion about the things of God and he will begin to move in your behalf.

Once you die to the need for something it no longer has power over you. Set your affections and watch the Spirit of God move.

Mercy Seat Message #219
"The Heavens Declare It"

We find it helpful to remind ourselves as to why we worship and serve the Lord. Yes, he has done a lot for us. He has blessed us, and continues to prosper the works of our hands. For those acts of his graciousness we are thankful.

He has certainly shown his love to us by healing us and helping us to maintain good health. In fact the thought of him saving us to be used in his awesome plan to redeem mankind makes him certainly worthy of our praise.

Recently though I had an opportunity to stroll along the ocean and stare at the horizon. The sheer vastness of the tiny fraction of the waters that I was gazing at began to overwhelm my sensibilities. The deafening roar of the waves as they crashed with untempered violence against the craggy rocks made me pause. The shimmering flash of the blinding sun made more than just my eyes wince. Can you hear and see it?

Well if you can, then you may have had the same thought I did. Maybe the starting place is to worship him just because of who he is. He is the creator of those vast depths of water, the endless sky that is its canopy, the multitude of animals and organisms that live within its bounds, the sun and stars that hang above it all...and on and on.

Yes, he is worthy to be praised.

Mercy Seat Message #220
"The L-I-F-E of God"

One of our popular praise songs is the one that goes... "I have the life of God in me...." Comprehending that life on a consistent basis is the key to maintaining your joy and avoiding depression, frustration and anxiety. Here's an easy way to remember the life of God. It is a

- **L** - oving Life: comprehending the nature of God's unconditional love for you changes everything about you. He has fully accepted you and made you righteousness the blood of Jesus.
- **I** - nspired Life: you can live in full confidence that no challenge is too great for you (through him) to overcome. In fact, you seek after challenges as the Lord leads you to higher heights and deeper depths.
- **F** - aithful Life: we serve a God whose own righteousness is based upon his faithfulness to his own promises. When he says you can do all things-he means it. When he says he will never leave you or forsake you-you can take it to the bank!
- **E** - ternal Life: knowing you are an eternal creature redefines the nature of this earthly life. Joy is easy to maintain because even the worst situation is temporary, even the most desperate condition can be redeemed. There is a constant knowledge that the best is yet to come.

If today isn't going the way you'd like it to-shake off those grave clothes and put on Christ. You have the life of God in you!!

Mercy Seat Message #221
"Where the Action Is"

You can imagine the shock of the religious leaders when Jesus told them that if they looked on a woman the wrong way they had committed adultery, or if they had designs on someone else's goods they had already committed a theft.

You see, the action in the Kingdom of God is deeper than just our behavior. Certainly we need to choose to refrain from sinful ways but even beyond that, the Lord is looking for purity of motive and of thought.

It is critical that we take to heart the admonition to "cast down vain imaginations". Don't let your mind wander today toward ugly or perverse thoughts. When you find yourself drifting, take those thoughts "captive" and be obedient to the Christ.

Your reward will be a constant sense of God's presence and that reassuring knowledge that there is nothing going on in your heart that would limit your ability to receive the love and blessings that the Lord is constantly causing to abound your way.

Mercy Seat Message #222
"From Mess to Miracle"

The scriptures make it clear that we should choose the path of blessing in every situation we are confronted with. It is plainly evident that we should follow after obedience in each circumstance we find ourselves in. With most of us, even our best efforts to live this way only end up demonstrating to us our even greater need for Jesus.

The marvelous thing about the love of God is that when we get off track, repent, and redouble our resolve to embrace our righteousness, our messes soon turn into miracles. We have all probably created an 'Ishmael" (moving in our own strength rather than waiting on him) but if we repent, an "Isaac" will come forth (that which He has promised us).

So if you're sitting there today in the middle of a mess...repent. Give it to him and watch the power of God work to bring forth your miracle.

Mercy Seat Message #223
"His Purposes"

Romans 8:27-28 encourages us that *"all things work together for good for those who love God and are the called according to His purposes".* On any level this is an incredible promise for it assures us that God will use even our faults and failures to produce blessing in our lives.

There is a way, however, to achieve even greater joy and blessing. That is, to see all things working towards our fulfilling God's plan for our lives because 1) our "love" is the action of obedience to that which God speaks to us as we seek him regularly, and 2) it is <u>his</u> purposes, not ours, that we are called to.

Go to him for each step of today's journey asking Him to establish his purposes in all you do. This will guarantee all things working together for good. It will also bless you with a heart- peace you may have never known before.

Mercy Seat Message #224
"Hand-Picked"

One of my finest childhood memories is the fresh-baked cherry and apple pies my grandmother would make for Sunday dinner. She would take such special care when she went into the garden to get just the right fruit. In fact, one of the signs of my maturation was when she would finally trust me to know which fruit to pick.

Not wanting to mess up the pies I would apply her exacting standards to each cherry---just the right firmness and free of any mold, and each apple--no softness on the outside and a stem that would easily disengage when gently tugged.

In this way God has chosen you for salvation and for the work of redeeming all creation. (Romans 8). No matter how imperfect we feel the truth is that he used exacting standards in selecting you and I because of the critical nature of the work that must be done. Just like my grandmother's, pies not just any fruit will do. It had to be handpicked. It had to be you.

Mercy Seat Message #225
"The Blessing of Forgiving"

The whole of the Bible emphasizes the blessing of forgiving. Just like you and I were blessed by God forgiving our sins, we are even more blessed when we forgive the transgressions of those who hurt us. In fact the less we 'deserved' the hurt, the more profound the blessing if we can forgive. The principle is a simple one.

Jesus suffered the consequences of our wrongs when He didn't deserve it. That gave him his crown of eternal glory. When we participate in his sufferings, the Bible tells us that we also then participate in his glory. Here's one thing that may be important to some of you on a purely human level.

Forgiving doesn't mean living with the idea that someone who wronged you "got away with something." That feeling that an injustice has gone unabated can be hard to handle emotionally. But the Lord says that vengeance is His, He will repay. He simply doesn't want you or I to be the ones to bring the guilty to justice.

Take some time to reckon with any areas of unforgiveness in your life. Ask the Lord to remove the need to "pay them back" for what they may have done to you. And then pray for them, so that any root of bitterness that may have grown up in your heart can be removed.

It is hard to forgive when you feel that the one who hurt you "got away with it". The feeling of being robbed, wronged, and taken advantage of can be unbearable. Understand though that no one "gets away with" anything. The Word tells us in Romans 12 that the Lord will do the avenging for you. He just wants you to get out the way and let him handle it rather than you getting wrapped up in revenge and vindictiveness.

So imitate Jesus. Forgive and be blessed...eternally.

Mercy Seat Message #226
"Heaven-Bound"

Imagine for a moment being exactly who you are now.... same good things about your personality, same positives of the way you think, same good relationships with family and friends.... all without the limitations of your body. Imagine flying instead of walking. Imagine never catching the flu, never getting tired, never being sad, depressed, hungry, or in pain. Imagine in this blissful state...never dying.

To many this may seem like weird fantasy or super-spiritual nonsense. Yet it essentially the condition that the Bible describes as being what heaven is like. We're not suggesting that you should be in a big hurry to leave. On the contrary, the certain knowledge of this eternal future is the sustaining force that enables you to have joy in the face of life's trials. It is also the source of hope that powers the ministry the Lord has prepared for you to perform.

To live without that hope must be difficult. But praise be to God that we can live with the knowledge that we are heaven-bound.

Mercy Seat Message #227
"The Joy of the Lord"

In our culture's spiritual emphasis on "happiness" we can miss something even greater...joy. While being happy is a state of mind largely ruled by circumstances, joy is intended to be mental condition, beyond the grasp of circumstances.

We are told in Hebrews that Jesus was willing to endure the agony of crucifixion because the joy of doing the will of God, and seeing us come into the kingdom, made it tolerable. We too need to see satisfying God's claim on our lives as a sufficient source of joy to melt away the stresses of life's ups and downs.

Your strength to face tomorrow does not therefore lie in your own capacity. It comes from an inward knowledge that has convinced you that the Lord has already taken tomorrow's problems and turned them into eternal praises.

Mercy Seat Message #228
"Understanding God's Authority"

The controversy of the universe is centered on who shall have the authority. To maintain God's authority we must be subject to it with all our hearts. It is absolutely necessary for us to meet God's authority and to possess a basic knowledge of what it is. Watchman Nee was a great thinker, and once said, "Let us not see the man but only the authority vested in him. We do not obey man but God's authority in that man."

In I Peter 2:13 & 14 the word encourages us to submit ourselves to every ordinance of man for the Lord's sake: whether it be the President or the Governors, etc. They are sent by him for the punishment of evildoers and for the praise for them that do well.

Therefore, it is important to know that God has ordained those in authority over us. Our focus should be the authority of God in that person rather than their attitudes faults and conduct. Hopefully, knowing that it is God 's authority will make it easier to submit. Remember all authority is God's and he blesses those are keen enough to discern it.

Mercy Seat Message #229
"Have An Out-of-the-Body Experience"

Being in the body of Christ is great—to be surrounded by believers exercising the power of the Word is wonderful. Once we have drawn from its strength, we need to get outside of the body and rub shoulders with the world.

Jesus' ministry was directed at the "lost sheep" of the house of Israel. Paul, and the other apostles eventually, brought the good news to the Gentiles. The focus was to get outside of the sphere of familiarity and reach those who had not been reached.

Jesus never participated, advocated, or agreed with the lifestyle of the lost. He spoke the truth in love and met them where they were, in order to elevate them to where He was. Go, and do likewise. It is the "darkness" that is most in need of the light.

Mercy Seat Message #230
"Everything With Nothing"

A favorite saying of Bible teachers is that the Lord can do "some" with a "lot", he can do "much" with "little" and "everything" with "nothing". There are times when we look at what we have to offer the Lord and it seems so insignificant and worthless. Be encouraged that whether you lack education, finances, or standing in society it is your heart attitude that will determine how much he can do through you.

Remember the loaves and fishes? Somewhere between the broken pieces falling in the basket and Jesus' prayer to the Lord, the "little" was multiplied. Remember then to give him what you have so he can break it. Remember also to commend it to the works of is hands in prayer. Remember that is for others that your "nothing" will do "everything".

Mercy Seat Message #231
"The Order of Loves"

The great 4th century theologian, St. Augustine, wrote about the "order of loves". He suggested that the priority of "God first" in our lives was critical because it was the only way to insure that our "loves" were correctly ordered. Anything other than God as our first love would wreak havoc on our lives because all other things would be out of balance.

Take for example the problem of alcoholism or drug addiction. If someone "loves" alcohol, all other things-spouse, children, job, friends-become subordinated to the love of drinking. And when one is an alcoholic their whole life eventually falls apart, not just because they are drunk (they usually function better when inebriated) but because their "loves" are out of balance. And all the other things are lost (taken away).

The same is true for all of us though perhaps not as easily visible as the alcoholic. If there is anything else above the love of God and the keeping of his commandments through faith in Jesus Christ, then our lives will also be out of balance. Jesus told us plainly to seek first the kingdom of God and all these other things would be added.

Mercy Seat Message #232
"Here I Am."

It is important to always remind yourself that you were saved for a purpose. The Lord chose you to be His righteousness because He had a specific role in mind for you to play in his plan to redeem all creation back under his sovereign hand. The work of the enemy is to first distract you from your purpose and then to feed you lies about your unworthiness to carry out that role.

In the 6th Chapter of Isaiah the prophet gets a glimpse of the holiness of the worship around the throne of Almighty God. He is immediately convinced of his uncleanness when one of the angels shows him he has been purified from the altar of incense, the prayers which go up on our behalf to the Lord. Isaiah's response to the removal of his guilt and sin is to make himself available to carry out the work of the Lord.

In an even more dramatic way the blood of Jesus has performed the work of those coals on the altar. Our sin and guilt has been taken away. The Lord is calling out in these days of tribulation-"Whom shall I send? and who will go for us?" Because of the grace and goodness of God our quick response needs to be as Isaiah's- "Here I am. Send me."

Mercy Seat Message #233
"An Advocate With the Father"

In wrapping up our series on "Renewing Your Mind", we made reference to our having an "advocate" for situations in which we fail to measure up to the fullness of the stature of the nature of Christ.

Imagine if there were a heavenly courtroom where, daily, Satan exposes all of your shortcomings before a Righteous Judge. This time the devil is not lying; his accusations of you are all true. The Judge must rightly dole out the punishment fitting the crime.

Just as sentence is about to passed your 'Advocate', Jesus the Christ, the Righteous, steps forward to plead your case. Though you may be at fault there can't possibly be any punishment because no man can be sentenced twice for one crime. "I've already paid the price for his sin", says the Advocate. The Judge nods in approval, looks at you and says, "Case dismissed. You're free to go."

Mercy Seat Message #234
"The Power Of A Vision"

In the 15th Chapter of Genesis God makes a covenant with Abram after painting him a picture of his promise. The Lord takes Abram outside and points him toward the sky, revealing to Abram that his children will be more numerous than the stars.

The interesting thing to note, as you read on, is that it was broad daylight when the Lord gave Abram the vision by pointing him to the stars! Although they were not visible amid the brilliance of the sun, Abram of course knew they were still there.

So it is with many of the Lord's promises to you, whether it be the restoration of your health, the wholeness of important relationships, or the fulfillment of ministry. You may not be able to see it, but if he has shown it you, he wants you to know that it is there.

Mercy Seat Message #235
"Sowing Seed"

A recent message on "sowing seed" was an important reminder about the power of our words and the reality that they can create. Our words are the containers of our thoughts. Thoughts reflect the condition of our heart.

To say that "today is a lousy day" is no less true than saying "I know the Lord can make something good out of the rest of this day". The difference is simply a heart that is not focused on faith and one that is. In fact, words can also work in reverse. You can create a heart condition just as easily. Keep telling 'Johnny' that he'll never amount to anything and chances are he won't. Tell him he can be the best he can be and he probably will.

Lots of things will come your way today. Think before you speak, even to yourself, and sow seeds of love, power, and victory.

Mercy Seat Message #236
"Many Infallible Proofs"

The Gospel writer Luke emphasized his understanding of the reality of Jesus by stating there were many "infallible proofs" that testified of him. These proofs were simply the demonstrations of Jesus' power and deity as he poured out God's mercy on those around him.

When you and I face trials today we need also to remember the "infallible proofs" of God's love for us. For every problem we will deal with today, how many others has God's mighty hand already solved for us? For every seemingly impossible obstacle we will encounter, how many times has he shown us that nothing is impossible for him?

If faith is evidence, then you and I are filled with faith, because we have lots of evidence of the Lord's love and desire to deliver us from evil. Lift up your eyes unto the hills from where your help comes. It comes from the Lord.

Mercy Seat Message #237
"Things Hoped For"

The Scriptures tell us that *"faith is the evidence of things hoped for..."* From the life of Abraham they drew out the important truth that if the Lord promises a thing it is the foundation of hope in our hearts from which we can exercise faith.

Despite Abraham and Sara's age, God's promise of a son came to pass. You may however feel like Abraham did at one point... nothing seems to be happening in terms of his promise to you and you feel the need to take matters into your own hands.

Rest assured that the Word of the Lord is true. At all costs avoid the temptation to take matters into your own hands. Don't produce that 'Ishmael. Wait for 'Isaac'. Let hope bring forth faith and wait on the Lord to make it all come to pass.

Mercy Seat Message #238
"God's Garden"

If you've ever tried your hand at planting a garden you know the care that it takes to ensure that something beautiful springs up from the ground. Once the seed is planted it has to be watered regularly and get enough sun.

No sooner than the tiny sprouts emerge, weeds invariably surround them. These weeds have to be removed regularly as well, as they often seem to grow faster and easier than anything else.

God has planted a garden in our hearts and he is intent on seeing that something beautiful springs up. He wants to water you with his word and warm you with his love. And if the weeds threaten your growth he will carefully pull them up to give you space to breathe. You are God's garden, and he is the gardener. Let him do what he needs to do to produce an eternal harvest in you.

Mercy Seat Message #239
"Waiting On The Word"

Living in an "instant" society has its advantages for sure. Whether it's quick-cooking rice, direct deposit or email, getting it "now" can be good. There are times, however, when it doesn't work so well. Like with the word of God.

The time between when the Lord speaks something to you, and when he fulfills it, is often not an 'instant'. It seems as if God's sense of time is way different than ours. Unlike minute rice, he believes in soaking, seasoning, and simmering until the time is right to bring forth in us what he has willed even before the world began.

We have great need of patience, the Word tells us, and if you are waiting for the fulfillment of God's word to you, take heart. He is the author and finisher of your faith, and the good work he has begun he will complete.

Mercy Seat Message #240
"See The Power"

We really need to activate the power of God in our lives, much like batteries in a flashlight.

Looking at a battery there's no way of knowing that it has power in it and can do things with that power. Likewise, there is no way that your friends, family and co-workers will get to see the power we have in Jesus unless we activate it and show the world what he is like.

Isaiah tells us in prophesying the coming of the Messiah that..."*The people that walked in darkness have seen a great light: they that dwell in the land of the shadow of death, upon them hath the light shined.*" Be that light and let people see the power.

Mercy Seat Message #241
"What You Love"

Like Abraham, at some point we may all have our faith put to the test of obedience to God's will and purpose in our lives.

After waiting years and years for a child, Abraham and Sarah were finally blessed with a son, Isaac. The Lord asked Abraham to sacrifice Isaac for a number of reasons; one being that it was one of the things that Abraham loved. Abraham was willing to obey because he knew the Lord would not take away that which he had promised.

As you and I go through the process of sanctification God will ask us to give him what we love. It may be your wealth, your knowledge, your children, or even your fears. He will ask for the thing you love the most as a sacrifice to him. Take comfort though, what remains will be greater than that which he desired from you, and he will greatly multiply that which he returns.

Mercy Seat Message #242
"Making the Connection"

In what we have come to know as the Lord's Prayer, we are told to confess that *"thy kingdom come, thy will be done, on earth as it is in heaven."*

In other words, one of the keys to prayer is simply manifesting God's kingdom-being intercessors for that which has already taken place in heaven to take place on earth.

That can be an entirely different prayer than the one we pray when <u>we</u> want something to happen, whether or not we know that it's something that the Lord has ordained should happen. It is said that Jesus always prayed the 'perfect prayer', that which was the will of the Father.

When you pray, spend time getting to know the Father's heart. He will tell you how he "feels" about the situation so you and I can pray in concert with his will in heaven. Present yourself as that channel through which his will can be done on earth. Present yourself as a vessel willing to be used to make a connection.

Mercy Seat Message #243
"Building the Body"

Scripture tells us that Jesus is coming for a 'bride'-a church without spot or wrinkle. While the truth of what is happening in the church is not the negativity often portrayed by the media, we do have a lot of work to do. As the Book of Nehemiah depicts we need to work together to restore the walls.

Although every expression of the Body of Christ has great validity, Jesus is not coming for a denomination, or a doctrine, or dogma. He is coming for a body that is fully prepared for the task of eternity. Depending on how you read Acts 3:21 it may be that he is waiting for the restoration project to be completed <u>before</u> He comes.

While Nehemiah inspired the people to rebuild the walls, we may need to inspire each other to tear down a few first. The things that separate our various churches and denominations that do not touch on the essentials of the faith should not get in the way of our fellowship. If they are going to know us by our love, then we need to find every opportunity to show it to ourselves.

Mercy Seat Message #244
"Handholding"

Psalms 37:23-25 says.."*The steps of a good man are ordered by the LORD: and he delighteth in his way. Though he fall, he shall not be utterly cast down: for the LORD upholdeth him with his hand.*"

We often focus on our rightful need to reach out and hold on to God's 'unchanging' hand, and while it's a good thing to do, there is so much more in the Lord. The scripture really speaks to him holding onto <u>your</u> hand, in a grip of grace that cannot be loosened.

Know today that, because of grace, the Lord <u>wants </u>to hold your hand, and will not let go of you in any circumstance. If you stumble, he will be there to steady you. If you fall, he will lift you up. He will set you back on your path because he has already ordered your steps.

Mercy Seat Message #245
"The Food That Endures"

In the 6th chapter of John, Jesus multiplies the loaves of bread and the fish to feed a multitude of hungry people Somewhat understandably, the people then seize upon the Lord, more for the food than for the opportunity to be in his presence. Let me suggest that this as an example of what we should be aware of as believers.

Naturally we all have needs. And in his marvelous way the Lord provides for those needs. But the point of our relationship with God is not what he can do for us. The point is the relationship itself.

You are encouraged to seek after Jesus "as" the food and not to seek him "for" the food. What he can provide for you will be used up as the need is met. What he is to you is the food that endures.

Mercy Seat Message #246
"Working It"

In Philippians 2 we are told to work out our salvation with fear and trembling, for it is God that is working in us to will and to do of his good pleasure. Naturally in our walk with the Lord we are required to put forth effort. Often, however, that effort is translated into "working hard" to receive and activate the blessings of our salvation.

In fact, the word "work out" actually has the connotation of "performing fully". In other words, working out your salvation has more to do with simply exercising the power, freedom, and purpose of the new creation, which we have been made to become, rather than exerting effort to be a better new creation! Whatever exertion is required of us is based upon our being obedient to what God has called us to do as those who are saved.

You can't overlook that last part of the scripture. It is God that is supplying the energy and he's doing it according to the direction he has set for you, for his good pleasure. If you really want to work it out then obey the voice of the Lord and submit yourself to his purpose for your life.

Mercy Seat Message #247
"Don't Be Fooled"

From many different corners of our society many different 'gospels' are being preached. One common denominator is that they all suggest that standards of morality and conduct are flexible and cannot be derived from any one source. The Book of Jude tackles this issue in his warning to the early church, to avoid false teachers.

Like Balaam there are many today who are saying that since we have the blessing of salvation, why bother with holiness and godliness? Why not 'enjoy' your time here since eternal life is assured? There are yet others, in the mold of Korah who incite rebellion at the authority of the scriptures as the rule of conduct. Still others, who have gone the way of Cain, resent the purity of the offering given by believers who attempt to exemplify that conduct.

Don't be fooled. The preachers of these 'gospels', as Jude says, are trees that will never bear any fruit. Their efforts to adapt morality to the rules of the culture is, in Jude's words, evidence that they are lost and headed into further darkness. Don't be fooled. Keep yourself in the love of God. Obey his instructions. Pull someone else out of the fire.

Mercy Seat Message #248
"If It's Blessed...It Can't Be Cursed"

In Numbers 23 that same Balaam is encouraged to curse the children of Israel. As much as he wanted to do so, even he realized that whatever God has put his blessing upon cannot be cursed.

As children of the Most High God we have his eternal blessing upon us. Eternal, because he chose to uphold you from the moment he conceived you, before the foundation of the world. As we walk in obedience and repentance, no circumstance, no matter how it may appear, has the power to remove that blessing.

Many 'prophets' may come your way this week. They will prophesy doom, failure, and inadequacy upon you. Unfortunately for them, they are not even as smart as Balaam. They will not realize that they cannot curse what the Lord God Almighty has already blessed.

Mercy Seat Message #249
"What You Do With What You've Got"

Matthew 25 relates the parable of the talents. The essence is that those who invested what they were given received a reward, while others who were afraid, held on to theirs. The parable tells us that those who were afraid actually had that which they had <u>taken</u> from them, while those who invested were given more.

We are all given different talents, true, but we are all given something. The sad thing in the eyes of God is when we despise what we have been given because we don't think much of it. Or worse yet, we compare ourselves with others to the point that we fail to see the value of what we have.

Unfortunately to do anything less than invest in what you have is an affront to God. The point is not what you think of yourself, but that you realize that if God gave it to you, then it is good, it is powerful, and it is vital to the plan of redemption. Ultimately then, it matters not what you have. All that matters is that you do something with it.

Mercy Seat Message #250
"The Path To Peace"

Everyone wants peace in their lives, it seems. To have health, wealth, friends, and all the pleasures of life, is almost worthless if you have no peace. But what really is peace in the Kingdom of God, and how do you get it?

Biblical peace is not the absence of conflict but the absence of confusion, even when conflict is present. As lights in a dark place and salt in a tasteless culture, you should probably expect a little conflict. But you should also expect to have peace....provided you meet the qualifications.

There will be little of this peace in your life if there isn't obedience to the direction the Lord has given you. You cannot expect there not to be conflict <u>and</u> confusion if you are not walking the path he has set before you. Looking for peace in your life? Obey the path that he has set before you and peace will find you.

Mercy Seat Message #251
"Weakness Made Perfect"

While we all know we are not 'perfect', we can often overreact to our imperfections. We can be far too conscious of our shortcomings, which can limit our sense of our ability to be used by God.

In 2 Corinthians 12:9 Paul says that when he is weak the power of Christ rests upon him. The word 'rest" actually translates into the Lord 'building a tent and dwelling' there in the midst of that weakness. In other words, when God calls you to do something and you lack the ability, the Lord will "set up house" and live there to complete whatever lack or shortcoming you possess.

There may be any number of things that the Lord has spoken to you to do, that this fear over your lack of capability has forestalled. It is quite common for him to call us to that place of incapability for the very purpose of being that strength through us. Perhaps it's time to get out of the boat and walk on the water. Perhaps it is time, as Paul says, to glory in your weaknesses.

Mercy Seat Message #252
"Gain By Losing"

Money is important to all of us. We need finances to attend to all of the details of life. The key for us as believers is to have the right attitude about money.

Oddly enough, the key to financial prosperity is all about an attitude that is completely counter to our instincts, and foreign to the thrust of our American culture. In our culture we are encouraged to desire things and then motivated to hold on tightly to what we have. We multiply it by placing it in tangible investments. If you pick the right investment, your money may well grow, and you can get what it is you desire. (Lately it's been difficult to find even these types of investments!)

As believers however, we are told to do very much the opposite. We are instructed to 'die to' the thing that we want, that is, to dismiss the craving and hunger for anything but that which the Lord wants for us. We then are instructed give our money 'away' by putting it into the intangible investment of the Kingdom of God. The difference here is that the Kingdom is always the right investment and your money will grow well beyond your expectations. With the right attitude, it will grow to the point where you can meet the needs of others as well as your own.

Mercy Seat Message #253
"Stewards Vs. Owners"

When the New Testament talks about material prosperity, wealth or riches, the context is that we are "stewards". Literally, a steward is someone who is responsible for overseeing the management of another's household. He or she takes care of the details of someone else's home and is accountable to them for how they do their job.

That's a lot different from being an owner. An owner can make his or her own decisions and is only accountable to themselves. It's that way with money in the Kingdom of God. What the Lord blesses us with, simply is not ours. We don't own it. We are stewards, answerable to God for how we take care of his "household".

We need to remember that. We need to understand that being a steward takes away the entire burden of actually providing the resources. As we give faithfully to God he has agreed, as the owner, to provide for the household that he has placed us in charge of. When you look at it from that point of view, being a steward is a pretty good deal.

Mercy Seat Message #254
"The Secret"

In Ephesians Chapter 1 Paul tells us God has revealed a secret to those of us who are believers. That secret simply is that he has planned a time when he will bring all things to a point of consummation and put all things under the authority of Christ.

If you have been saved for any length of time, that secret has probably become "common knowledge" to you. It is a fact that you have probably accepted fully, and that has become integrated into your view of everything around you. Sadly, there are many in the

Body of Christ, and especially those who are unsaved, who know of no such "secret".

The impact of knowing that God has this remarkable plan is a big one. Life is no longer empty, mysterious, or purposeless. Fear, worry, anxiety, and depression are only passing experiences rather than a permanent state of one's existence. This is what makes our sharing the gospel so vital. People need to know that there is much more to life than what they see. They need to know that they are part of the plan. This is one secret you can feel free to share with everyone you meet.

Mercy Seat Message #255
"He'll Finish What He Starts"

While salvation is received when we ask Jesus to be the Lord of our life that is only the beginning. We are then brought through a continuous process of being conformed to the image and likeness of Christ. This is not just some spiritual-sounding phraseology. That process is a very real sifting and winnowing of those in our person and personality that need adjusting for us to fulfill the purpose we were saved for.

The comfort we have in this sanctifying work of the Holy Ghost is that it is his work. We need not strain and stress over the things that the Lord is shifting and remolding in us. The only 'work' is the bending of our knees and the bowing of our will to the decisions he makes for us.

Hebrews 12 tells us that he is the 'author and finisher' of our faith. He chose us to be adopted as one of his children and he will raise us up according to the rules he has established for his household. We only need to obey. If you are ever discouraged in your ability to see Jesus in yourself at times, take heart. What he started in us he will finish.

Mercy Seat Message #256
"Endure Hardness"

In 2 Timothy Paul tells the young minister to "endure hardness as a good soldier of Jesus Christ". 'Hardness' is the affliction that we encounter when we take a stand for righteousness. Much more than the persecution that comes from others or the tribulation that may swirl around us, it is the war inside our own hearts as we battle the enemy's attempts to dissuade us from our stand.

In fact, a 'soldier' as Paul uses the term is not just a follower in the army, but one who is tasked with enlisting others and leading a military expedition. That is why we can expect even more 'hardness' to be endured. Whenever you take the position of leadership you become an even greater threat to the enemy no matter who it is. Their ability to strike down the leader is intended to demoralize those committed to that leader.

There is always good news in the word of God. The Scriptures tell us that the righteous endure many afflictions, but the Lord delivers them out of them all. Never let the enemy cause you to forget that the battle is the Lord's!

Mercy Seat Message #257
"Transformed By The Word"

As we grow in the grace of God the process of sanctification is an ongoing work. The Holy Ghost is at work convicting us to allow God's holiness to take over more and more of our habits and thought patterns. Sometimes our growth in the ways of the Lord causes us to forget exactly how these habits and thought patterns get removed. We can easily slip into a form of complacency, believing that somehow the Lord will just "take them away".

What cleanses us, as Peter says, is the washing of the water of the word. God's word has the ability to reproduce his righteousness in us. But this doesn't just 'happen'. We have to read, partake, chew and digest the word if it is to have its desired affect. Remember the days when you found scripture that addressed your need for any type of deliverance? Remember how you would meditate on those scriptures until they became alive in you and the change began to manifest itself? What's different now that you know him even better? Nothing, except perhaps our focus and discipline in applying the principles that the Lord has taught us.

Need things to change in an area of your life? Still have some old-nature-immaturity rising up in your habits and thought patterns? If so, go back to the basics. Let his holy word transform your heart and mind. It still works!

Mercy Seat Message #258
"Operating As One Man"

Judges 6 and 7 tells the familiar story of how Gideon, and only 300 soldiers, defeated the army of the Amalekites who were "without number". Gideon was visited by the Angel of the Lord who assured Gideon that he would go ahead of him to bring him victory. The admonition was that Gideon was to operate as "one man" with the Lord.

As ministers of reconciliation, you and I need to abide in the Word, and in the presence of God, so that we are "consumed" like the offering Gideon made after his visitation. We need to have such a close relationship with the Lord that we "decrease' as he 'increases'. If you are attentive to this, then he will go ahead of you and direct you to be a vessel of encouragement, and even deliverance, for those in need.

The next time a friend, co-worker, or family member comes to you for advice or counsel, make sure you are operating as "one man". Submit yourself to the power of the Holy Ghost so that it is no longer you, but the Spirit ministering through you. Let the hands that touch them be his. Let the words that are spoken proceed forth from his very mouth.

Mercy Seat Message #259
"The Power Of Plurality"

All throughout Proverbs we are told that there is "safety in a multitude of counsel". The concept seems to be that when making decisions, leading the flock, hearing from the Lord, in virtually all of the things we do that have an impact on the equipping of the saints, it is preferable to have group leadership. The shared responsibility and mutual submission required of this "multitude of counsel" creates a protective climate for the will of God to be accurately expressed.

Interestingly enough many church ministry activities can become dominated and led by just one individual. Whether it is a pastor, a prophetic gift, or an anointed worshipper, we can fall into the trap of a "one-person" show. For example, the New Testament seems to clearly reflect that the churches were led by a group of elders rather than a single person. Among the functions that were given certainly included pastoring and teaching, but not as "job descriptions". They certainly weren't the ones that 'ran the show'.

Ephesians 4 tells us that we all are engaged in coming to the full knowledge, stature and mature expression of the Christ within us. We cannot afford to lapse into some sort of hierarchy where some people are deemed to have greater and more compelling gifts. There is only one revealing of the Christ and we all have to work together to see it in the Body of Christ and within one another.

Mercy Seat Message #260
"Something To Live For (Hope)"

Ever marvel at the amazing sense of expectation that children possess? They are often able to believe for things way beyond the boundaries of most people's imagination. There are hardly any limits to what they think is possible. Later, when the reality of adulthood sets in, common sense and the facts of our experience temper that expectation.

No one would be foolishness enough to suggest that we should live our lives like children, ignoring the limits of "reality". There is something to be said, however, for rekindling that sense of expectation that reaches for things beyond the boundaries. The Bible calls it "hope". It is the joyful and confident expectation based on God's ability to make things happen. It is a sad thing indeed to lose your hope, to have learned to settle for whatever has been your reality, regardless of something else that the Lord has for you.

Whether it is a less-than-inspiring job, a family that just doesn't seem to function well, or a financial situation that never seems to go beyond being in debt, or service in the kingdom of God that doesn't seem to be affecting anyone's life, all of these could use an injection of hope. Join me in asking the Lord to rekindle that sense of expectation that there is more for them than what they see in front of you. And if you are the one we are praying for, reach out with confident expectation and take hold of what the Lord has planned for you.

Mercy Seat Message #261
"Healing In His Wings"

Every Monday night the saints of the Global Truth Ministries gather for Intercessory Prayer. It is a time when we come to pray for the needs of others, many of whom we do not know personally. But they are the co-workers, sisters, brothers, nieces and nephews that have let one of our folks know that they have a need for prayer. It is not a time when we bring our own needs before the Lord but a time when we are believing that if we focus our attention on other people, he will meet whatever needs we may have. We consider it an honor and a special blessing to be used by the Lord to pray in such a fashion.

Of the hundreds of requests that come in we have seen a huge increase in people asking for prayer for healing. Cancer, diabetes, kidney failure...virtually every type of physical ailment is represented. We believe with all of our hearts, based on the Word of God, that the Son of God has arisen with healing in His wings. The New Testament indicates that while immediate, on-the-spot healing certainly occurs, much of it is "therapia", a progressive but constant process of release from "dis-ease". We have numerous praise reports each week of cases where this "dis-ease" has been lifted and the person we have prayed for set free.

If you, or someone you know, has a similar need, let us know. You may in fact be reading this and have yourself lost all of your ability to believe for your healing. But just as the paralytic was healed by the "faith of a few close friends" we are here for you as well. Email us at info@globaltruth.us or leave us a phone message at 703-539-6033. We'd love to pray for you or those you know. It's an awesome sight to see Him arise and his enemies get scattered!

Mercy Seat Message #262
"Children Are Like Arrows"

Psalms 127 tells us that " As arrows are in the hand of a mighty man; so are children of the youth". This scripture paints a vivid picture of the role we adults need to play in equipping the next generation to fight the good fight of faith. Whether you are a parent or not, we all have a hand in planting the seed of righteousness in the hearts of the children. In today's world this need seems to be rapidly escalating.

The evening news is full of condemning stories of the failures and faults of our young people. They have even been labeled as "Generation X" by marketers and advertisers, as a comment on their lack of focus and direction. The truth is that our children are just that-children. Their failures and faults are often just the reflection of a culture that has forgotten that their real needs cannot be satisfied by video games. They need encouragement, discipline, guidance, and love. They will seek any medium available to find these things if they are not found at home.

That's where we believers enter the picture. The kingdom of God, presented in a way that can be understood, offers anyone, young or old, the opportunity to receive what they need to thrive. We aren't talking about them just going to church, we need to be the church: a loving, open, accepting extension of Jesus himself, who welcomed the children to come to him, Don't be fooled by what you hear or read in the media. Our children are dying because they are looking for something to live for.

Mercy Seat Message #263
"Stewards Over A Number Of Things"

Of all the devil's insidious plots, the one that tries to get you and I to be "owners" rather than "stewards" is perhaps the most dangerous. A steward, as I mentioned before, is someone who takes care of, administers over, and manages, the assets of another person. This stewardship role is carried out with greater diligence than if the assets were the steward's own.

The Lord has made you and I stewards over a number of things- "...of God" (1 Timothy), "...of the mysteries of God" (1 Corinthians), "...of the manifold grace of God" (1 Peter). We are also obviously stewards over material things such as money or possessions in general. If we think and act as if these are our own, we fall into the demonic trap of taking God's place in the decisions we make regarding these things. We open the door to the lusts of the flesh and miss the blessings of generosity. The tighter we try to hold onto these things, the faster they evaporate. We question the need to obey God in tithing, thus questioning his authority over 10% of the 100%. It all already belongs to him and he has given it to us to manage for Him.

Being a steward requires faithfulness above all. Some people wait for God to enlarge them when they aren't even taking good care of the little they have. The scriptures make it clear that the ability to be a faithful steward over a few things is the prerequisite for being given much. Don't overlook the little things and don't act like an owner. Be a faithful steward and the Lord will bless you with abundance.

Mercy Seat Message #264
"Like Hinds Feet"

Psalms 18:33 reads, *"He maketh my feet like hinds' feet, and setteth me upon my high places."* A hind is a mother deer, one of the most sure-footed animals in the world. When she is going up the side of a mountain with her young following her, she takes her back feet and places them exactly where her front feet were first placed, to test for loose stones on the slope.

If she did not test the rocky incline with her front feet, the loose stones would cause her to slip and fall down into the ravine below. This exact tracking means life and safety both to the hind and to her young. This verse tells us that we can take God at his Word, because he has made the way safe for us. It tells us that where the Word has set its feet, we can take our stand on that spot.

Mercy Seat Message #265
"The Whole Armor"

Luke 19 records the parable where the master tells the servants to "Occupy until I come". The word "occupy" is a Greek military term referring to taking up a position in a hostile country. In like manner we as believers are given the task of occupying. This is a hostile word, saturated in sin. We are in it but not of it and are here to be its light and salt. Sounds like a real war zone, doesn't it? Well, in fact, you could make a real good case for this world being such a war zone and the Lord has given us the weapons to be victors in the fight . 2 Corinthians 10 says..."For the weapons of our warfare are not carnal, but mighty through God to the pulling down of strong holds;"

We are also given armor to sustain us in the battles we encounter. Ephesians 6 tells us ..."*Wherefore take unto you the whole armor of God, that ye may be able to withstand in the evil day, and having done all, to stand. Stand therefore, having your loins girt about with truth, and having on the breastplate of righteousness; And your feet shod with the preparation of the gospel of peace; Above all, taking the shield of faith, wherewith ye shall be able to quench all the fiery darts of the wicked. And take the helmet of salvation, and the sword of the Spirit, which is the word of God:*"

When you head out for school, the office, or to run your errands today, you will make certain to be properly dressed. You will have hat, coat, gloves, and even an umbrella, depending on the forecast. You will have your running shoes with you for that long walk from the office to your source of transportation when the day is done. Don't forget to wear your most important clothing. Don't forget to put on the whole armor of God.

Mercy Seat Message #266
"Beware of The Leaven"

In Mark 8 Jesus warned His disciples to beware of the leaven. He referred to the Pharisees and to Herod Anitpas, and in other scriptures added the Sadducees to the list. These groups symbolized various forms of distortion and deception. The Pharisees were seen as hypocrites, telling the people to do the things that they themselves were not willing to do. The Sadducees denied all aspects of the supernatural power of God including heaven, hell, angels, spirits and even resurrection. Herod Antipas, who, along with Pilate would condemn Jesus to the cross, probably represented the influence of worldly wealth and political ambition.

While we need to have strict adherence to the Word of God we have to also practice what we preach. While we have to be grounded in the reality of our walk with God we must also reckon with, and recognize, the spiritual realm, a level of consciousness beyond our five senses. And while material prosperity and influencing the culture are part of our commission as believers, we must stay true to God's will and purpose in these things and not get sidetracked.

"A little leaven", as Paul said, "leavens the whole lump". A little bit of hypocrisy can discredit your influence over the unsaved people who watch you everyday for signs of the reality of your faith. A little too much human reasoning can limit your ability to be used by the Lord to bring answers to a hurting friend or family member. A little too much ambition, or failure to seek the kingdom of God first, can negate your own blessings. Beware of the leaven. Be student of the Word. Do and say, not much more than what you hear and see, from our Father in heaven.

Mercy Seat Message #267
"The Fruit Of Conflict"

The word 'conflict' literally means, "to strike together". In most instances we perceive it to be less than positive, due to the emotional and mental stress that can accompany conflict situations. While there is no way around this potential for stress, it is important to see that conflict may not only be necessary, but essential, in bringing forth that which the Lord has ordained in our lives.

When the apostles met in Jerusalem in Acts 15 there was a huge conflict ("no small dissension") over what regulations to impose on the new Christians in terms of Jewish law. The outgrowth of that was a new liberty in the application of God's grace, especially for the Gentiles. In this instance an uncomfortable clash was the opportunity to bring glory to God and to birth his plan for the salvation of all men. Their paradigm for how God was going to move among them was changed.

This example may not seem relevant to you in your daily lives but here's the point. Birth does not occur without conflict. The striking together of your will and God's will can produce an uncomfortable feeling in your heart-*you know better than to fight against God but you can't accept what he wants for you either.* In these circumstances remind yourself that something is being birthed-a new direction, a new depth of anointing, a new dimension of revelation. Do what every expectant mother learns to do at that moment of crisis-breathe deep, hold on to someone who loves you, and push.

Mercy Seat Message #268
"The Cave Of Adullam"

In 1 Samuel 22 David is hiding out in the cave of Adullam, trying to avoid conflict with Saul. While he is there, people hear about where the real King of Israel can be found. And as it says in verse 2, *"And every one that was in distress, and every one that was in debt, and every one that was discontented, gathered themselves unto him; and he became a captain over them: and there were with him about four hundred men."* These rejected ones later become a mighty army that drive the Philistines out and bring the Ark of the Covenant back to Israel.

In these days the Lord is also looking for such a people. Though they may not seem to possess much on the outside and may have endured some of the vicissitudes of life, they know the real thing when they see it. Not only do they know it, but they are wiling to go after it. They are wiling, in fact, to lay down their lives so that the

Spirit of the Lord can live through them so that his will is done on earth as it is in heaven.

There is a desperate need today to take back the "Ark" from the Philistines. So much of our culture is trying to rob the body of its vitality and make the Gospel seem irrelevant. So many issues within the church itself have tried to substitute the power of God's presence for political issues that can be voted on. We have tried to make Jesus palatable to a culture that does not want to hear words like "sacrifice, forgiveness, or commitment.". We have twisted the gospel to subtlety suggest that the entire price was not paid on the cross and that God is somehow still mad at you. Don't fall for any of that. Seek the reality of God's presence. Embrace a living relationship with the Lord. Visit him in the quiet place of your heart. Become one of God's mighty ones.

Mercy Seat Message #269
"Torah"

The word "Torah", as used by the Jewish people, is synonymous with the "Law", essentially the first five books of the Old Testament. Remember that the word literally means 'instruction'.

Anyone who has developed a familiarity with spiritual things knows there are forces at work, which the human brain cannot comprehend, and are in fact, counter to the way the natural mind operates. For example, to give away your money or possessions in order to see them increase, or to forgive those who do destructive things to you, are both counter to the way most of us think. Keeping the Law therefore has little to do with God trying to punish wrongdoing, and everything to do with him instructing you and I on how to avoid the consequences of our actions, at a level of operation that we cannot understand.

Idolatry, vain speech, disrespect of authority, violating the principle of the Sabbath...all have dire consequences, not just on us as individuals, but on our households, extended families and the society in which we live. We must be careful as a society not to elevate our intellectual capacity to a place where we question why God says what he says. As a household we must be cautious not to evaluate God's directives on the basis of what makes sense to us.

As individuals we must altogether avoid allowing our emotions concerning the things of God, to be the barometer of our willingness to obey.

Mercy Seat Message #270
"Remember The Sabbath"

You may have had a similar childhood experience when Sunday was a day when nothing "fun" could be done. No baseball games could be played, no games of chance, hardly any activity was allowed. Stores were closed and only a precious few people had to report to their jobs.

What is interesting is that the Biblical definition of "work" and our concept of employment, are not really the same. Actually the commandment is referencing God's six days of "creating" the world and "altering the environment". It is this definition that even today guides the decisions of Orthodox Jewish people who keep the Sabbath with religious acts. That's why a rabbi can teach on the Sabbath but can't turn on a light switch or drive a car. The conducting of a service is not a creative act, even though it is employment. But using electricity or a combustion engine is a creative process because it alters the environment.

So what are we to do and not do on the Sabbath? Well for one, the commandment says to 'remember'. Remember that you are not the creator. Remember that although your mind tries to convince you that you are, and should be, in control of our environment, that you are definitely not. Remember that your salvation is a free gift and you can't 'work' to earn it.

Mercy Seat Message #271
"Thou Shalt Not Commit Adultery"

For something to be 'adulterated' it means that it has been polluted by the addition of ingredients that do not belong in the mixture. Based on this understanding one can see that the commandment concerning adultery is much deeper than just the prohibition against a physical act. God has ordained marriage as a unique and sacred channel for his anointing to flow through. It is a mysterious union where two very different people begin to function as a spiritual union. It is the basis of the numerical and spiritual growth of a community, based on the keeping of a covenant. When ingredients that do not belong are added to it, the explosion reverberates throughout the community.

It is clear that the church especially does not understand the power of a covenant. When two people marry they enter into an agreement with God to allow him to direct the course of the union. They enter into a covenant with each other to honor and obey their promise to God. Their two families enter into a covenant with each other. Even the community, which is present to witness the union, enters into a covenant with all of the above to support and help the couple to preserve their covenant.

If we understood all of this we would protect all aspects of a marriage with much more vigilance. The penalty for adultery was death to all involved. Whenever a commandment requires death as the means of restitution, that tells you that the sin has taken life out of the community, and there is only one way for it to be replaced. In this instance we have an even larger issue. While we need to be concerned about all sex sins as a blight on the kingdom of God, one might maintain that adultery has done more to weaken the church than homosexuality will ever do. If we were as vigilante about adultery in the church, as we are about homosexuality in society, you might wonder what sort of power the church might have over the world.

Mercy Seat Message #272
"Thou Shalt Not Commit Adultery"
-Part 2

James 4:4 reads " *Ye adulterers and adulteresses, know ye not that the friendship of the world is enmity with God? whosoever therefore will be a friend of the world is the enemy of God.* " This passage creates a somewhat different definition of adultery. It is not the physical act that James is referring to, but it still one that pollutes a covenant.

All throughout the scriptures, both Old and New Testaments, our relationship with the Lord is described as a marriage. Israel, for example, was admonished over and over again for its harlotry, the Lord having wedded them to himself. In the New Testament, the Body of Christ is to be presented to Jesus as a spotless and wrinkle-free bride. James is reminding us of how critical it is to not establish a covenant relationship with the desires and passions of our human flesh, and to seek their satisfaction by those things which the world offers.

There are many other ways in which the friendship (covenanting) with the world can lead us to be unfaithful to the Lord. For example, everyone needs a level of esteem. The key however is not to allow your job, or your identity at work, to be the source of that esteem. You should feel good about who you are because of who he made you to be not because of how important you are in the world. Having been created in the mind of God, before the foundation of the world, to accomplish a purpose in the earth that only you can accomplish, should be more than enough to feel valuable, and to have that necessary sense of importance. Remain a friend of God and avoid friendship with the world.

Mercy Seat Message #273
"Throw Her Down"

In the books of Kings you may have read about the story of Ahab and Jezebel. Ahab is recorded as one of the most wicked kings in Israel's history, bringing the worship of the heathen god Baal into prominence. His wife Jezebel, however, was an even more frightening force of wickedness, whose very threats scared the prophet Elijah. Jezebel was the daughter of a heathen king and a prophetess of the cultic religion that worshipped Baal.

Eventually, the word of the Lord spoken by his prophets came true, and the power of Ahab's house was destroyed. It takes the courage of new King Jehu, however, to bring Jezebel's reign to an end. When Jehu confronts Jezebel two eunuchs throw her down from the tower and she meets her demise. Two eunuchs, huh?

What this may be saying is that the forces of darkness that attack our lives, and the lives of our loved ones, are best dealt with by those who are not subject to their own physical passions. To be free from envy, pride, lust, jealousy, covetousness, and all those other like vices, may be the best antidote to the ills that plague us. Another way to put it might be to say that the forces of darkness will find no place to manifest themselves in those whose lives that are filled with God's holiness.

Mercy Seat Message #274
"No More Training Wheels"

Remember when you were first learning how to ride a bicycle? Either you chose to start with training wheels or just figured you'd jump on see what would happen. For those of us who chose to jump on and give it a whirl, a telephone pole, mailbox or other immovable object, may have been the first stop. But after a few more tries we eventually got the hang of it, counting the bumps and bruises as part of the process. This can be a lot like walking with the Lord.

Without much training in spiritual things some folks just want to jump out there and give it a go. The hurts and frustrations don't cause them to stop pursuing the things of God. They just count it all joy, as part of the process. The training wheel approach can be just as good, although it had its own set of issues. For one, if the person who attached them to the bike didn't do it right, you swayed back and forth as you tried to ride. It was also kind of tough to turn sharp corners.

The worst thing though was getting so used to them that you were afraid to take them off and really ride. It can be like that too, with spiritual things. We can sit in church for years, listening to the word, and hearing about all the things that are going in the kingdom of God. We're getting good training for sure, but at some point we need to get out there ourselves and do the work we keep hearing about. For many of us that time has come. It's time now to take of the training wheels. It's take time to take them off and give it a whirl. Time to take them off and really ride.

About the Author
Rev. LeRoy Thompson, Ph.D.

Rev. LeRoy Thompson is the Senior Pastor of Global Truth Ministries in Springfield, Virginia. He is a gifted Bible teacher with a passion for revealing the truth of the innocence that Jesus provided to us by his death, burial, and resurrection. He and his wife Rita have served as missionaries in Kenya, Uganda, Mexico, and Haiti.

He has a heart for outreach and taking the message of the gospel outside the church walls. This has led to him performing jail and prison ministry, coaching collegiate sports, serving as a Fairfax County Virginia Community Chaplain, and teaching parenting and fatherhood classes. He is a certified Master Trainer for the National Partnership for Community Leadership's "Fatherhood Development Curriculum." LeRoy also conducts the Fairfax County Public Schools Family And School Partnership's "Dads Matter Class" and is a parenting program instructor for the County's Department of Family Services. He is certified in Critical Incidence Stress Management and Pastoral Counseling Intervention.

LeRoy was educated at Harvard University where he received a Bachelor's degree in English and American Literature and Language, and a Master's degree in Finance and International Business from Columbia University Graduate School of Business. LeRoy received his Doctor of Divinity from Master's International School of Divinity and his PhD in Biblical Studies from Trinity Theological Seminary. He has done Talmudic studies at Yeshivat Har Etzion (Israel).

As a bi-vocational pastor, he has also operated an independent management consulting practice in corporate strategy and organizational development.